JOSEPH BLENKINSOPP, S.D.B.

THE CORINTHIAN MIRROR

A study of contemporary themes
in a Pauline epistle

SHEED AND WARD
LONDON AND NEW YORK

FIRST PUBLISHED 1964
SHEED AND WARD LTD
33 MAIDEN LANE
LONDON W.C.2
AND
SHEED AND WARD INC
64 UNIVERSITY PLACE
NEW YORK 3

© JOSEPH BLENKINSOPP, S.D.B., 1964

IMPRIMI POTEST: Thomas W. Hall, S.D.B.
Provincial

23rd April, 1964

NIHIL OBSTAT: JOANNES BARTON, S.T.D., L.S.S.
CENSOR DEPUTATUS

IMPRIMATUR ✠ GEORGIUS L. CRAVEN,
EPŪS SEBASTOPOLIS, VIC. GEN.

WESTMONASTERII, DIE 4A MAII 1964

This book is set in 11 pt. Linotype Times

*Made and printed in Great Britain by
William Clowes and Sons, Limited, London and Beccles*

CONTENTS

Dedicated affectionately to
the Salisbury Branch of the
Newman Association

FOREWORD

THESE short chapters were not written as a commentary on 1 Corinthians. The reader will not find any systematic exposition of the text and hardly any philology; and many of the exegetical issues which take up much space in commentaries on this letter are either not touched on at all here or passed over rapidly. The idea has been to provide some sort of basis for a consideration and discussion of themes, of some aspects of life in the Church, which are of permanent and practical importance in our lives today as they were, under different circumstances, in those of the Christians of Corinth nineteen centuries ago. It is hoped that this thematic presentation, even though incomplete and selective, will facilitate biblical thinking (or rethinking) and discussion in a way not easily realized just by consulting the commentaries.

Why 1 Corinthians? At first reading, it might seem to present some rather formidable problems, such as the discussion of Wisdom at the beginning, as well as quite a selection of irrelevancies—baptizing for the dead, meat offered to idols, women's headgear in church. Yet this letter is used in the Liturgy more than any other of Paul's, with the sole exception of Romans, which, although certainly more compendious, speculative and profound, is also much more difficult. Corinthians, written a year or two earlier, is more immediate and contemporary in flavour. It speaks of the problems of the everyday and the concrete difficulties involved in realizing the potentialities of the Christian life in an intractable situation— and therefore it can speak with persuasive power to us also. It is full of that indefinable sense of Christian consciousness which is primarily a Church-consciousness, a sense of *belonging*, and an all-pervading optimism and joy. It should therefore be a good antidote to that isolationism and subjectivism, and above all that sense of frustration, which are so characteristic of the spiritual life of our century.

Another reason for choosing this letter for a rather more detailed and thorough approach to Scripture is that we can very easily go on from here to a wider and more general reading in the New Testament. Passages such as the rule on divorce, the eucharistic tradition, the summary of Paul's preaching, provide vital links between the life of early Christian communities and the four written Gospels, while, on the other hand, we can go on more easily to study the development of Paul's thought in the other Epistles once we have become well acquainted with one of them. Some ideas for a thematic study of this kind will be found in an appendix at the end.

We read in the Epistle of James of the strange case of a man who, having once seen himself in a mirror, goes away and forgets what he looks like. There is something of a parable here for the individual Christian or the group which has allowed itself to lose contact with the word of God, since it is only by looking in this mirror that we can realize our own identity as Christians. This short study, which owes a debt of gratitude to many people of different Christian groups who read and love the Scriptures, was written with the purpose of contributing to that work of realization and self-understanding.

New York, October 1963

INTRODUCTION

1

FOR a Christian who knows something of his history a journey through the Middle East today can be an unnerving experience. Of the once breathing and vital organism, the Church which animated all that eastern seaboard and the inland regions, there is left little more than the bones picked clean by time. Matter, it would seem, chiefly for the archaeologist and palaeontologist.

After reading the tremendously lively and optimistic story told in the Acts of the Apostles the contrast is particularly marked. Antioch, from which the first Christian missions went out, has only a derelict and crumbling barn of a church and no resident priest; the theatre at Ephesus, where the mob demonstrated for two hours in honour of Artemis threatened by the bringers of a new cult, is now ruined and empty and the harbour silted up; and the country within whose boundaries all the ecumenical councils of the first thousand years of the Church's history took place now has a token Christian force. Philippi, where Paul's words about Christ's self-emptying and exaltation were first heard, is now a rarely visited ruin along the road from Kavalla to Drama in Thessaly; Corinth sleeps in the haze among the oleanders, and the same hand has been laid on nearly all those Churches which he founded and which were once flourishing Christian communities. The battlefield has changed and time has passed them by.

Our concern today is not primarily with archaeology or palaeontology, yet it is to that time and to those Churches that we have to go back in order to assess our present position, our losses and gains, and to see in which direction we have to move. For the Christian, this can best be done by reading the history of these early communities in the Acts of the Apostles. Originally the second part of a two-volume work composed by Luke, a second-generation, non-Jewish Christian, it was probably first separated from the story of "all that Jesus began to do and to teach" in the second century, when the need began to be felt for a fourfold Gospel under one cover. It was fairly common at that time to write the "Acts" of famous men—Alexander or Hannibal for instance—and the author was quite familiar with contemporary literary procedures. The story opens in Jerusalem with that small body of frightened men and closes in Rome on the eve of the first great persecution. The Acts of Peter and, to a lesser extent, of John, occupy the first chapters, but it is not until ch. 8, the dispersal of the Hellenist Christians and the first mention of Saul, that we begin to move abroad. This was a real turning-point, because it resulted in the founding of the Church at Antioch, a far greater city than Jerusalem (in fact, the third in the Empire), which was to become the first real missionary centre. Luke has preserved for us the names of the first Church leaders of this community, the first to be called Christian (a disparaging title used as a nickname); they included a Cypriot, a North African (possibly two), a Palestinian and a Cilician.[1] The visitor of today, arriving in this city, now called Antakya, perhaps after a hair-raising ride from Iskenderun (the zigzag road littered with the skeletons of cars and lorries), might find it difficult to picture the affluence and glitter of the first-century capital set splendidly on an impregnable height overlooking the vast and fertile Hatay as far as the sea, a centre of political and social life, famous for the Groves of Daphni, haunted by innumerable courtesans. It took a long time for people to take note of this new group in their midst and longer still, no doubt, for them to pick them out as a separate "synagogue" from the considerable Jewish community. As Deissmann says, "The Christ-cult was in the time of Paul a secret affair of humble, unknown people in the back streets of the great Mediter-

[1] Acts 13.1.

ranean cities."[1] But small as it was, it had something to say to the world and was determined on having a hearing.

It was to this city that Paul was brought from his native Tarsus by Barnabas, a Jewish Levite of Cypriot origin. He was then perhaps about forty. His family had close ties with Palestine, "the old country", but Paul was reared in the ghetto of Tarsus, once a fine university city, then a little past its best, now a small and not very clean village clustered round its mosque beside the River Cydnus, upon which Cleopatra sailed to meet Antony in a golden barge. He had gone up to Jerusalem at an early age for his training as a rabbi and must have been associated with the Cilician synagogue that our author mentions.[2] He would already have had to learn by heart a great part of the Scriptures by *viva voce* repetition, as one can still hear orthodox children doing in the Jewish city of Jerusalem. His further initiation into the traditions was carried through "at the feet of Gamaliel" whom we remember to have urged moderation on his colleagues in the Sanhedrin in respect of the new movement. His distinguished pupil does not seem to have followed this course, for we find him taking part in a

[1] Adolf Deissmann, *Paul: A Study of Social and Religious History* (1912), Harper Torchbook ed. (1957), p. 56.

[2] Acts 6.9.

violent demonstration against the Hellenist group in the early Church, probably during the period immediately following Pilate's recall in A.D. 36. But just when this reaction had reached its climax this Pharisee rabbi underwent a shattering experience somewhere on the road from Jerusalem to Damascus. The story is familiar and is told, in all, three times in Acts. This was the decisive turning-point in the history of the early Christian community, for Paul emerged as the foremost among that Judaeo-Hellenist group who were the first to see clearly the universal dimensions of the message and, above all, of the *fact* of Christ, and follow it up in practice. After a stay in Damascus, during which he retired for a time somewhere in the Syrian desert to think over the implications of his conversion, he made his first visit to the Apostles in Jerusalem[1] and thence went via Caesarea to Tarsus, where Barnabas found him a year later.

In the course of a liturgical gathering some time during Saul's twelve-month stay in Antioch the community decided to embark on a missionary expedition. This was entrusted to Barnabas and Saul was appointed as his adjutant. There were probably others, but we have the name only of John Mark, cousin of Barnabas. This missionary journey simply followed the pattern of the pro-

[1] Acts 9.26; Gal. 1.18.

selytizing and missionary endeavours of Dispersion Judaism which had been going on for some time. Jews were numerous and sometimes prominent in every part of the world in the first century; in Alexandria, greatest city after Rome, there were three-quarters of a million and we know of almost two hundred synagogues throughout the Roman world from either contemporary references or archaeology. There was sporadic but intense anti-Semitism, as witnessed by Claudius' letter to the Alexandrians (in the year 41), references in Tacitus and Suetonius and indeed by Luke himself. In fact Claudius, about the year 50, expelled the Jews from Rome, which was the fortunate occasion of Paul meeting Aquila and thus gaining a *pied-à-terre* in Corinth. It is noticeable that Barnabas and Paul, and later Paul alone, always looked for the synagogue when they entered a strange town and began their missionary work from there—as a rabbi he had a right to speak; this also explains why he uses rabbinical procedures so often and the apologetic approach of Dispersion Judaism of the kind which we find, for example, in the Book of Wisdom.

It is possible that originally only a preaching mission to Cyprus was contemplated. Whatever the case may be, they crossed over to what is now Turkey, landing probably at Antalya and pushing on and up into the Toros Mountains, while John Mark, for some reason which has given rise to much learned speculation, returned home to Jerusalem. This rugged country of tree-clad mountains and great cobalt lakes, now characterized by its scattered and squalid villages, its camel-wrestling and the desolate cry of the muezzin, gave Paul his hardest test to date. His experience there also showed him that it might be necessary to break with the Synagogue, though the definitive breach did not come until Corinth. The company returned the same way they had come, only to find that in their absence a major crisis had arisen over the admission of non-Jewish converts into the Church. Here takes place what is sometimes called the Council of Jerusalem, at which a compromise was agreed on which left Paul free in practice to continue as before. He therefore, on his return to his base at Antioch, set off on a kind of pastoral visitation of the new Churches, accompanied this time by Silas. We do not know what his plans were after that, but something happened in the course of the journey which led him to carry on north and west until he came to Troas in Mysia below the Hellespont. Here he had the vision of a young man, whom he recognized by his dress to be a Macedonian, inviting him to cross over the hundred miles of water into Macedonia. Here also begins the series of extracts from a travelogue in the first person which covers a good part of Paul's adventure story.[1] Paul accepted this strange invitation—not, we might suppose, without some apprehension.

For us there is something momentous about that moment when their ship warped into the busy little harbour of Neapolis after a day's sail from Samothrace. For this is the first occasion which we have definite word of, and which we can therefore visualize, when the good news about Jesus came to our continent. It may be doubted, however, whether Paul and his friends saw it that way. In thought, in pattern of life and culture, the world was much more closely integrated then than it is now, though of course much smaller. Greek thought had from the beginning been deeply indebted to the East; scientific thought first saw the light along the Ionian seaboard, Pythagoras's teacher was a Syrian, Plato's religious mentors were from the East. Thus there would not have been the feeling of something new and strange, as there would be today in passing from Europe to Asia or vice versa.

Paul's first stop was at Philippi, a Roman town settled by veterans of the civil wars, in contact with Rome by means of the Egnatian Way, one of the great highways of the ancient world much used by Paul. In that city he set up, amid the

[1] The Western Text, fuller than the one behind the text we are familiar with, includes a short passage in the first person at 11.28 apropos the prophet Agabus in the Church of Antioch.

usual troubles, a Christian community which was to remain in many ways the one nearest to his heart. By now, however, the opposition was organized, and he had to move on to Salonika. From there once again to Beroea, in the hope of getting back soon; but once again his enemies caught up with him and there was nothing for it but to take the sea-route to Athens, where he could wait unmolested until it became possible to go back north and continue the work which had been interrupted.

It is here that Paul's real stature shows. He might have waited at Athens for the all-clear, kicking his heels until he could return. Paul, however, was not the man to kick his heels or be afraid of getting involved. That, in fact, is what happened. We shall have to come back later on to the intensely interesting experiment in apologetic or, better, dialogue, that Paul attempted among the philosophers of that rather jaded but still very important intellectual centre.[1] Enough for the moment to record that he failed; there is no letter to the Athenians, no Church was founded and there is no evidence that he returned. As his chances of getting back to Salonika receded, he went on across this isthmus to Corinth, a disappointed and despondent man. It must have been about the year 50.

[1] See Appendix 1.

2

After two earthquakes, in 1858 and 1928, the
old city was abandoned and a new one built three
or four miles to the north-east. Its strategic position on the isthmus *made* Corinth and determined
its character such as we find it by reading between
the lines of the letter. There was, of course, no
canal in Paul's day; both Alexander and Caesar
had plans to build one and Nero got as far as
setting slave gangs at work, the marks of whose
premature toil are still visible. The present four-
mile-long ditch, disfigured by a horrible little iron
railway bridge, was finished in 1893. In Paul's
century ships from the East were unloaded at
Cenchreae and then hauled (on rollers) across a
prepared track called the *diolcus*, still visible, to
be reloaded at Lechaeum and sent on their way
to some Italian or African port. In a society
which reposed like an iceberg upon a great mass
of submerged slave labour, this solution presented
no special problems.

Little of the Corinth which Paul saw as he
walked or rode in from Cenchreae has survived
the intervening two thousand years. For the
visitor who walks across the now quiet *agora* the
whole scene is still dominated by the great rock,
the Acrocorinth, upon which stood the temple to
the Goddess of Love where, in Strabo's time two
centuries before Paul, a thousand courtesans had

practised sacred prostitution. That was before the Romans burned the town to ashes, but even after it was rebuilt a century later, in 46 B.C., there was little change. It was the capital of Achaia, a province which took in most of present-day Greece, and we should remember that the letter would have been read far beyond the bounds of the city. For one thing, we know that there was a small Christian community or Church in the Eastern port of Corinth, Cenchreae, in which Paul had his hair cut in accordance with a vow he had taken. By a happy chance one of the deaconesses of this Church is known to us by name.[1]

At the time of Paul's visit Corinth was governed by the proconsul Gallio, brother of Seneca, a fact mentioned by Luke and confirmed by the Delphi inscription discovered at the beginning of the century. Despite being the capital of a senatorial province, however, the city remained in every way typical of the Eastern Mediterranean. All kinds jostled in its markets: Nubians selling ivory, merchants from Thyatira with dyed cloth, others just back from conquered Britain (there was an altar to Victoria Britannica) with gold, jet and tin.[2] Corinth was also the site of the Isthmian

[1] Rom. 16.1. Her name was Phoebe.
[2] Throughout the whole of the New-Testament period, especially in Acts, there is a juxtaposition and mixture of races, trades and social classes which is truly astonish-

Games, second only to the Olympian Games; these were held every other year and brought in plenty of trade. We have no means of knowing whether they were held during Paul's stay and whether, if they were, he took time off to see them, though 1 Cor. 9.24–7 might suggest that he did. More to our immediate purpose, we know from archaeology that a "Synagogue of the Hebrews" stood on the Lechaeum Road in a crowded residential area, and it must have been here that the Jewish colony lived and that Paul settled. Luke tells us, in fact, that he eventually took up residence next door to the synagogue.

His first contacts were, as we have seen, with a Jewish family which had settled there temporarily

---

ing. As Henry Cadbury, a leading authority on Acts, puts it: "What mixed names and backgrounds have the people that Paul meets! The Roman proconsul Gallio was born in Spain (Cordoba), King Agrippa is of Idumaean descent, while of Paul's associates Timothy is half-Jew, half-Greek, Silas has both the Semitic name and the Roman name Silvanus, Barnabas has the name of a Babylonian deity but is a Jewish Levite. Perhaps as a Cypriot some Phoenician blood flows through his veins. Aquila is a Jew of Pontus formerly resident in Rome and with a Roman name, while Apollos is an Alexandrian Christian with a reputation for Greek eloquence or learning who still taught the baptism of John. Such a world needed a universal religion and a missionary who could be 'all things to all men'." (*The Book of Acts in History*, London, A. and C. Black (1955), pp. 28–9.)

after having been obliged to leave Rome as a result of the imperial edict. Several other Corinthian Christians are known to us by name—in fact, quite a list could be drawn up. A glance at these names shows what we might have expected —that many of them were Roman. The community's headquarters seem to have been in the house of a certain Stephanas. There must have been a good number of them—Luke tells us there were "many",[1] and they were numerous enough to split off into factions (1 Cor. 1.10ff.) and seem to have been drawn from many different walks of life, some of them "men with a past". Paul had to worry over the problems of so many different kinds of people; not just stevedores, factory workers and shopkeepers, but people with some education, both slave and free, people who were in the habit of getting invitations to banquets or being mixed up in legal entanglements—not to mention the inevitable pseudo-intellectuals, the neurotics, the bossy and eccentric women. It is precisely for this reason that the letter is so fascinating and so relevant for us still. In fact, it would not be too much to say that the general situation of that Christian community in a rather sleazy city poised between East and West with a good mixture of races, social classes and temperaments, has quite a lot in common with many

[1] Acts 18.8.

Christian communities in a world nineteen centuries older.

3

There are one or two things about the way the letter was written which ought to be borne in mind if we wish to avoid unnecessary puzzles. Paul was not an academician and he rarely had the leisure to produce a finished and polished literary work. During the three-year stay at Ephesus, when he was in intermittent correspondence with his Christians at Corinth, he was constantly on the move throughout the province of Asia, of which Ephesus was the capital; he was not infrequently in serious trouble and hardship, and more than once in danger of death. Yet all this time he supported himself by working at his trade and when saying goodbye to the elders of the church could hold up his hands to remind them.[1] His letters, then, must have been dictated between times, mostly, no doubt, in the evenings. Even supposing that he had occasionally a longer period of time at his disposal, an amanuensis cannot carry on writing indefinitely, and there must have been many intermissions, some of them long ones, especially in this letter, which was the longest he ever wrote. Add to this the fact that we cannot be certain that everything here is in

[1] Acts 20.34.

the order in which it came from his secretary's hand, and it will be obvious that this is no theological treatise.

There are two canonical letters, but this evidently was not the sum total of the correspondence which passed between Paul and the Corinthian Christians during the time that he was staying at Ephesus. He refers in our letter (5.9ff.) to a misunderstanding which had arisen from something he had written in a previous exchange. Then delegations had arrived from Corinth; we know of one from some of the household of a woman called Chloe, apparently of some standing in the community, bringing news of the different parties which were beginning to spring up and also, perhaps, of a grave public sin which had been committed. (1.11; 5.1–8.) Stephanas, who may have been the leader of the community in Paul's absence, also came to have some moral problems cleared up. All this called for treatment in writing, and this we find in the First Epistle to the Corinthians, written probably about Eastertime of the year 57 in the expectation of soon being able to visit them. As a result of a new crisis in the community (there seemed to be no end of them) this visit was brought forward but proved to be very brief, with the promise of a longer one at a later date—communications between the two cities were easy and the journey would not normally take more than three days.

At this point, however, he seems to have been insulted or had his authority impugned (2 Cor. 2.5–10; 7.12), as a result of which he cancelled his visit and sent them a stiff letter instead (7.8–13), which has not survived unless, as some think, parts of it are embedded in the second canonical letter. After receiving news that they had reacted favourably to this scolding he wrote again, and this is the second canonical letter. It comes from the last period of his long stay in Ephesus and is full of references to what he had to suffer and put up with in that city.

This means that reading this letter is rather like listening to a telephone conversation at one end of the line and trying to fill in the gaps. Unfortunately, some commentators and many more preachers have forgotten this and have distorted what Paul is saying by taking it as a treatise or a series of treatises written without hurry or interruption by someone sitting at a desk surrounded by books of reference. The very style of the letter should have warned away from such a conclusion. It is direct, conversational, full of either rhetorical or point-blank questions (there are ninety-six of them!)—rather like a preacher talking to his congregation; and, in fact, Paul's letters were intended to be read to the whole *ekklesia* gathered together at the service of the word of God, and when writing them he visualized his Christians together in plenary assembly.

What we have to bear in mind is that the letter is really a series of answers to questions not all of which are easy to reconstruct. One example will suffice, one to which we shall return. If we were to set about putting together a theology of the married state from this letter we should be rather disappointed—all rather negative and discouraging. But of course this letter does not contain any such theology. We shall of course, as always with Paul, find valuable insights, but what he is doing here is answering such questions as, Since the Lord is coming soon, wouldn't it be better not to get married at all? Or, My pagan husband was not converted with me and is making my life as a Christian well-nigh impossible—what do I do? And so on. Out of this material, and other questions (such as regulations about Jewish food laws) which have only academic interest for us today, we can deduce Paul's underlying moral attitudes and persuasions—and this *is* something of the greatest interest for us. It is also, incidentally, a good example of the process, not always easy, by which the word of God to Christians of the first century becomes the word of God for us in the twentieth.

4

Here we come up against a problem which every intelligent reader of the Scriptures finds

himself debating sooner or later—what we can
call the problem of relevance. Such an enormous
volume of water has flowed under our bridges
since this Jew of Asia Minor dashed off the letter
we are considering to an insignificant community
in a Levantine town—can we still honestly accept
it as saying something to us, men and women of
the twentieth century, which is significant for our
lives? To start with, the way we understand our
environment has been revolutionized since Paul's
day. Not only our understanding, but also our
control, is immensely greater. Take the question
of space. Our world is so much larger than Paul's,
despite the truly staggering distances that the great
Apostle travelled. This means that we can
appraise more realistically the question of the
universal salvific plan of God. There is quite a
lot of evidence in Paul's letters that his perspective
on this question changed considerably during his
ministry. In the earlier Epistles, of which this is
one, the coming in glory of the risen Lord is
clearly in the forefront of his mind. His increasingly painful experience of obduracy and opposition on the part of the Jews led him without a
doubt to reconsider this eventuality, since (as it
clear from Romans 11, especially *vv.* 25–6) there
must be a time of salvation for the Jews after the
Gentiles have come in. Moreover, in the later
letters the expectation of his own death enters
more and more into his direct field of vision. Nine-

teen centuries later our perspective will be different again.

If our world is larger than Paul's, what of the universe in which that world is only an infinitesimally small grain of matter? Is not Paul's gospel vitiated by the very terms in which it comes to us, based upon and presupposing what Rudolph Bultmann calls "the cosmology of a pre-scientific age"? The drama which lies at the centre of the gospel is played out upon a stage with three storeys—heaven, earth and hell—a scenario which is an integral part of Jewish apocalyptic but which is for modern man the product of pure phantasy. Can we really expect people to accept a gospel which makes such huge and unwarranted demands upon their credulity? Does not, further, the whole idea of salvation and a heavenly saviour depend for its validity upon the prior acceptance of such a view of the world—when Paul gave the Christians of Philippi the picture of a divine being pre-existing above in glory, coming down below for a time in self-abasement to return to his place of origin, was he not reproducing the saviour-myth familiar all over the world in his day?

This is of course a huge and complex question, much discussed, much popularized, much misunderstood in recent years. Though it came very much to the forefront of discussion after the appearance of Bultmann's manifesto on the need for demythologizing the New Testament in 1941, it has in fact always been with the Church in one way or another and quite a chapter of biblical interpretation could be written on the *Entmythologisierung* carried through by early ecclesiastical writers. For what in fact Bultmann is doing is what has been attempted in every vital period of Church history, namely, to state the Gospel in terms of a philosophy intelligible to the men of that day. One of this great scholar's most acute critics has in fact written:

> Bultmann is doing something analogous to what St Thomas Aquinas did in his day and generation. Just as Aquinas worked out a rapprochement between Christianity and Aristotelianism, so Bultmann is at any rate outlining the possibility of a rapprochement between Christianity and existentialism. The basic issue at stake in the *Entmythologisierung* is whether such a rapprochement is either possible or desirable.[1]

We can go further than this and state that this process of trying to penetrate to the real meaning of words, terms and formulae was already in existence during the New-Testament period. It is altogether too naïve to suppose that Paul, for example, does not see the implications behind the analogical language which he uses when he speaks

[1] I. Henderson, *Myth in the New Testament*, London, S.C.M. Press (1952), p. 22.

of God and the divine activity, or to take it that
he understands heaven and hell, to take a familiar
instance, as precisely located, the one above, the
other below. A good test of this keen sense of dis-
crimination is to read the exhortations in the
Pastoral Letters to preach the *word*, that is, the
truth incarnate in historical reality, and eschew
the "myths and endless genealogies" of those
gnostic Jewish converts who had already begun
the process of explaining by explaining away.

A greater practical difficulty is the dimension
of time. Is it being realistic to ask people in the
name of the Gospel (and these letters are nothing
but the Gospel passed on) to regulate their lives
on the supposition that any day Christ will return
and bring us face to face with the judgement of
God? Do people—Christians—really believe that
the final world catastrophe is imminent? There
have been, of course, at intervals, people who have
believed they could pinpoint the day and the hour,
but they have invariably and correctly been taken
as cranks. Nor does the general preoccupation
with the Bomb affect this feeling of irrelevance.
Since we shall be coming back fairly frequently
to this vital point at different stages of our reading
of the letter it will be enough to give here an outline of the context in which this question has
to be answered. Many Christians at Corinth
evidently thought of Christ's coming in glory as
imminent. Did Paul share this view? He speaks

2

of them "waiting for the revealing of our Lord Jesus Christ" (1.7); he provides for the saving of the spirit of the immoral Christian "in the day of the Lord Jesus" (5.5)—a technical term for judgement; he speaks of the distress, which is always in Jewish thought the harbinger of final judgement, as imminent (7.26); he says that the appointed time to run before the end has grown very short and that the form of this world is passing away or about to pass away (7.29–31). These and similar expressions must be given their full values. At the same time, Paul knows very well that the appointed time is hidden with God and states so clearly in writing to the Christians at Salonika. He may ardently hope for it, he may think he sees signs of it approaching, but he knows that Christ has said, "Of that day or that hour no one knows, not even the angels in heaven, nor the Son but only the Father."[1] And then, as we have seen, his perspective gradually changed as time went on. The "Day" is seen in an increasing depth of focus which must allow not only for the completion of the redemptive mission of the Church among men—the Nations and then the Jews—but also for the completion of the world. Meanwhile the Corinthian Christians had at length to come to terms with their own death and try to understand it in the context of the death

[1] Mark 13.32.

and resurrection of Jesus,[1] and they are given a magnificent help towards their task in the explanation of the meaning of the resurrection of the dead. (ch. 15.)

Faith will always remain, seen from our level, a choice made in the presence of conflicting possibilities, confirmed by a decision implying final commitment. The enormous collective experience of two thousand years presents us with a greater range of possibilities and, to that extent, the approach to the initial act of faith may be more difficult today. But it is open to serious doubt whether even in that uneasy, post-rational age, when the gods were dead but still had to be appeased, the understanding of existence acquired by an intelligent citizen of Corinth who had, perhaps, pondered on Lucretius and frequented the Mysteries, qualified him, more than his counterpart in this century, for an easy acceptance of a specious message of happiness. It is because we share, after all, the same human nature, the same perplexities, the same problems, that this letter can still have so much to say to us.

[1] There are clear references to death, sometimes overlooked, in 1 Cor. See 11.30; 15.18; 15.29.

God chose what is foolish in the world to shame
    the wise,
God chose what is weak in the world to shame
    the strong,
God chose what is low and despised in the world,
Even things which are not, to bring to nothing
    things that are . . .
He is the source of your life in Christ Jesus.

We have received not the spirit of the world
But the Spirit which is from God
That we might understand the gifts bestowed on
    us by God.

You are God's field, God's building.

All things are yours
Whether Paul or Apollos or Cephas
Or the world or life or death
Or the present or the future;
All are yours
And you are Christ's
And Christ is God's.

THE CHRISTIAN'S VOCATION IN
THE CHURCH

THE mutual exclusion of Church and world is at the bottom of any right idea of Christian vocation in terms of Church membership and is often lost sight of now as at all times. It is a constant of the temporal mission of the Church, will always be present and, far from there being any hope of an eventual mutual inclusion, will go on being more clearly marked and defined.

Everything that Paul says to the Corinthians, the way he deals with every subject that crops up, presupposes that the Christian community is not and cannot be identified with the world. But what does he mean by "the world"?

The first thing to note is that the basic mode of Jewish and New-Testament thought is temporal rather than spatial. When early Christian theologians brought their minds to bear on the religious significance and destiny of the world their thought-patterns were horizontal more than vertical; time never had an absolute validity coexistent with eternity, of which it was a shadowy reflection. This was true of Greek thought, for which time was an endlessly recurring cycle which held no possibility of real progress. In the New Testament our kind of time measures our kind of existence—what is called "the present age". This is in the process of moving forward to its appointed end, to a catastrophe—understood here and throughout in its etymological meaning of "a decisive turning-point"—which would usher in a new age—"the age to come"—in which the rule of God would at last become a reality and not just a pious aspiration.

This semantic interaction between "world" and "age" has led to no end of misunderstanding, due especially to our tendency to transpose the temporal into the spatial. Thus our usual formula "World without end", which comes to us through the Douai's mistranslation of the Pauline doxology, is strictly meaningless, and when we speak in a more or less jocular way of "the wicked world" we are unconsciously making the same transposition. When New-Testament writers, and Paul among them, speak of "the world" as evil we must be careful to understand what they mean. Here again, our translations have not always served us well. A good test would be to read the first letter of John, which admittedly speaks of the world rather in the idiom of ascetical writers on the religious state who speak of leaving the world and entering religious life. There we read: "Do not love the world", "All that is in the world, the lust of the flesh and the lust of the eyes and the pride of life, is not of the Father", "Do not wonder that the world hates you", "The whole world is in the power of the Evil One"—and so on. The writer is not taking "world" in the Greek sense according to which the *kosmos* is evil because evil (that is, contingency) is built into it as part of the nature of things, which means that the religious man must *escape* from it in order to reach salvation. He is thinking of a definite *aion* or age, a world-order dominated by elements which are hostile to the development and fulfilment of the divine plan.[1]

But this distinction between "the present age" and "the age to come"—to use the terminology of Jewish apocalyptic—is not just a question of temporal succession. Even on the basis of our modern attempts to understand the nature of time we should suspect such an interpretation to be inadequate. In fact, the Christian reinterpretation of Jewish thought on this point is quite drastic. First, the act of God in raising Jesus, "the Lord

[1] See especially 1 John 2.15; 3.13. In view of the sometimes quite close verbal parallels between the Johannine writings and the Qumran Scrolls it is interesting that the latter, written by "religious", betray the same attitude with, however, significant differences. See F. Moore Cross Jnr, *The Ancient Library of Qumran*, 2nd ed., Doubleday (1961), pp. 209–10.

of Glory" (2.8) brings in "the age to come" and puts an end in principle to the "present age". The death and raising of Jesus is the decisive "catastrophe" and contains the ultimate self-revelation of God. The reason is that the raising of Jesus is not just survival of death, as was that of Lazarus and Jairuss's little girl or, for that matter, the two children raised to life by prophets in the Old Testament. It is a passing into a new and different dimension of existence not just for Jesus alone (this would make the whole of redemptive history unintelligible) but for Jesus as man, in so far as in so doing he reveals to us and makes possible a radically new dimension of existence. For Paul, the man in Christ is a "new creation"[1] precisely for this reason. Upon the Christian living in the Church "the end of the ages has come" (10.11) because it is in the Church that the new age is inchoate; therefore it is now open to the Christian in the Church to experience —by miracle, by the charismatic gifts and the experienced presence of the Spirit, by prophecy —"the powers of the age to come".[2] The decisive blow has already been struck against "the debater of this age" (1.20), "the rulers of this age" (2.6).[3]

---

[1] 2 Cor. 5.17; Gal. 6.15.

[2] Heb. 6.5.

[3] A great deal of effort has gone into determining what this expression means. It should at any rate be taken to include both human and superhuman elements in opposi-

The wisdom of the present *aion* has, by means of the Christian message, been exposed for what it is and made void. The Gospel is the chapter of a radically new epoch.

There is no question, then, of a straight opposition between the Church and the world as the environment in which the Church happens to find itself. There *is* between the Church and the existing world-order in so far as the latter is not a good vehicle for the realization of God's plan for mankind. It is in this latter sense that Paul speaks in our letter of the Church as constituted by a vocation to leave the world. It is therefore, in Newman's phrase, a community in process of separation from the world, a definition which is in all rigour deducible from the way in which Paul speaks to the Corinthians about themselves as Church members:

The word of the Cross is folly to those *in the process* of perishing, but to us who are *in the process* of being saved it is the power of God [present participle]. [1.18.]

---

tion to the divine economy. For Paul the world, in its aspect of negation and opposition, includes both human and superhuman agencies: "We have become a spectacle to the world: both to angels and men" (4.9) he tells them, and, later on, states that the judgement of the world by the saints will take in the angels also. (6.2–3.)

It is a natural deduction from this that Paul should speak throughout of the Christian in the Church by a series of antitheses:

> The spirit of this world ... the spirit which is of God. [2.12.]

> Natural man [belonging to this *aion*] ... spiritual man. [2.14–15.]

> To take thought for the world ... to take thought for the Lord. [7.32.]

The Christian, then, has a vocation to leave the world, not enjoined on him in the idiom of exhortation but by an imperative which is supported by arguments of great weight. The chief of them follows from what we have been saying about the world and is expounded at some length in the first part of the letter; namely, that the world is essentially the power-structure of society which consciously or unconsciously places itself at the disposal of the evil forces that rule the fate of natural man—represented sometimes in the New Testament as "elemental spirits"[1] which are somehow behind all the giant mechanisms of the natural order—the procession of the seasons and the heavenly bodies—into which the existence of man is remorselessly drawn. By his decisive intervention in raising Jesus from the dead, God has broken the stranglehold of fate and enabled man,

---

[1] Gal. 4.3; Col. 2.8 etc.

by becoming somehow part of that redemptive act, to find a way out to freedom and fulfilment.

As we read the magnificent and magistral passages 1.18–2.16 we may well begin to wonder whether civilization, culture as we commonly understand it, has any significance for the Christian or any legitimate or necessary point of contact with life in the Church. Here it is particularly important not to lose our perspective by taking this passage out of its context. Paul is preparing here to defend his simple and elementary catechetical instruction of his new converts in the face of the onesided attachment of many of them to the brilliantly speculative and profoundly theological approach of Apollos, who had arrived on the scene at a later stage and taken Paul's instruction a stage further. This key figure in the early Church is introduced to us in Acts 18.24–19.7. He came from Alexandria, home of Philo and the subtle and profound scriptural exegesis later to be adopted by the great Origen.[1] He had been received there but evidently by one of the disciples of John, a group which played a large (but as yet to us rather mysterious) part in the early history of the Church. He had come to Ephesus, according to tradition the home of the Fourth Gospel, and it might be more than a coincidence that that Gospel is so interested in

[1] Hence the hypothesis that Apollos was the author of the Alexandrian Epistle to the Hebrews.

the Baptist and his followers and contains more than one polemical note in their regard. After being "straightened out" by Priscilla and Aquila, he went on to Corinth and instructed there, evidently with the purpose of building on and elaborating Paul's more elementary catechesis. (1 Cor. 3.6.) It is natural, therefore, from all this, that the Corinthians, factious and over-speculative as they were by nature, should have tended to draw the wrong conclusions. But there is another reason more important still. When Paul says, speaking of his attitude of mind on his arrival at Corinth, "I decided to know nothing among you except Jesus Christ and him crucified", he is, without doubt, thinking of the attempt which he had made at Athens at expressing the Gospel in terms of an ascendant philosophy, in this case contemporary Stoicism, an attempt made with full knowledge of and sympathy with those with whom he entered into dialogue. The breakdown came with the mention of the raising of the dead body from the tomb, for this cut across the whole movement of Greek religious thought, for which salvation consisted essentially in escaping from the body and from matter. It seems that, as a result of this failure, Paul decided, at least for the time being, to abandon this approach and to concentrate on the stark and irreducible fact of the Cross—"the foolishness of God". (1.25.) Despite this, however, the attempt *had* been made and would in fact be taken up in the Church and pursued to its limits.

While, therefore, the Church has to grapple with philosophical views of existence which do not originate with her, there is something in human thought untouched by the redemptive act, left to itself, the empty play of the intellect—what Paul calls "the wisdom of the world" (1.20; 3.19) —which cannot serve the divine purpose. The reason is that there is always a relation, often undetected, between moral and intellectual life— a man does not think in a void. Writing somewhat later at Corinth to the Church of Rome in what is his greatest and most compendious statement on Christian existence, Paul would say:

> They are without excuse; for although they knew God they did not honour him as God or give thanks to him, but they became futile in their thinking and their senseless minds were darkened. Claiming to be wise, they became fools,[1] and exchanged the glory of the immortal God for images . . .

In other words, the validity of philosophy is affirmed; but on the social level, statistically, this process of thought, natural theology, had failed to clear a way for man out of his straitened condition. The result of this failure is that "the wisdom of the world" makes the working out of the

[1] Or, better, "morons"—*emoranthesan*.

divine economy impossible in the world. Hence the need to create a community set aside from the world, in which this plan of God can have free play.

This community is the Christian Church, and it is "to the Church of God which is at Corinth" (1.2) that Paul writes. Since the use of singular *and* plural occurs commonly and has no polemical significance we need spend no time on it, except perhaps to note that the individual "Church" is always reminded of its links of unity with the Great Church—"to the Church of God which is at Corinth... with all those who in every place call on the name of our Lord Jesus Christ"; with the sister-Churches of Achaia (Greece), such as Cenchreae in the first place, with the Asian Churches, in a special way with the "Churches of Christ in Judaea"[1] which served as models or prototypes for the others.

It is always a good thing to start by looking hard at the meaning of the word itself. The Greek *ekklesia*, derived from the verb "to call", means the sum total of those who are called forth. It was used in a political sense for a plenary assembly of citizens—thus the demonstrators in the temple of Artemis at Ephesus are called an *ekklesia*, a "church" or assembly. (Acts 19.32.) The theological significance lies in the underlying implica-

[1] Gal. 1.22.

tion that the Christian assembly in any given place is made up of those who are called out of the world, who have therefore received a call from God. So the Corinthians are invited to consider their "calling" (*klesis*, from the same verb), and just as the apostle has received a vocation and is therefore called by God from the generality of men,[1] so are Christians "called" (*kletoi*) from the world. (1.2.) The other epithet which Paul very often places alongside this, "holy", really boils down to the same thing. The Christian is called from the world into a holy union with God as Abram was called from Ur and sent on his long pilgrimage out of *his* world, but "holy" should be taken in its original and basic sense of apartness, sacrality, separation, dissociation from what is profane. This is true of the word in its primal sense in Hebrew, Greek and Latin. It is in this sense that the often misunderstood designation of "saints" is often used in early Christian literature.

Christian Church membership comes about, therefore, by a vocation to leave the world. Absolutely antecedent is the grace of vocation which comes from God. It is not like membership of a club or society, to which we subscribe after having weighed up the pros and cons. Paul begins by thanking God for *the grace* given to the Christians

[1] See, for example, Rom. 1.1; 1 Cor. 1.1.

at Corinth through Christ Jesus. (1.4.) Later on, working out his great statement on Christian existence to the Romans (ch. 5), he will refer to "the grace in which we stand". It is, further, characteristic of the divine action in this regard that there should be no proportion between the merits or excellence of the one who receives and what he receives. This is a major biblical theme, as can be seen by reading carefully the narratives of the call of Saul, David and other Old-Testament figures. It was true of the Twelve, as is clear from the Gospels, it was painfully true of the first Christians of that sophisticated and disreputable city: "Not many of you were wise according to worldly standards, not many powerful, not many of noble birth . . . " (1.26.) There is, evidently, an ineradicable, diametrical difference between God's way of acting and that of men. There is no point of comparison or intersection. God does not act on what is there already; his action is always creative, and therefore unprecedented and unpredictable. When he makes his choice among men he chooses "the things that are not" (1.28) to raise up a people for himself as he raised up one long before from the dead womb of Sarah.[1] His way of acting cannot be questioned or subjected to scrutiny. It can only be accepted even in the absence of guarantees, or rejected. The

[1] See Rom. 4.16ff.

Church is therefore the area where the action of God and the response of man meet: "It is of him that you are in Christ Jesus." (1.30.)

At this point we should note that the instrument for bringing the Church into existence is the proclaimed good news of God, the Gospel, what Paul calls elsewhere "the word of faith"; and, since the heart and soul of this message is what God has done in the death and resurrection of Jesus, "the word of the Cross". (1 Cor. 1.18.) Word and Church cannot be separated and will always be unintelligible if taken separately. If we read Paul's analysis of the process of *becoming* of the Christian community in Romans 10 we shall see the force of this and how this living and dynamic view of the Church must underlie any ideas we may have of her as an organization. From this point of view we can have no quarrel with the Reformers' definition of the Church as existing "wherever the word is preached and the sacraments administered"—for that is precisely what we find in Scripture.

Church and world are, then, two spheres which do not and cannot intersect. The Christian is different. Church membership is not just our ordinary lives plus one or two extras such as going to pray (or just kneel or stand) in a certain building once a week, going to confession now and again, being respectful to priests, nuns and others of that sort. It is, on the contrary, a new and radically different kind of existence, different right from the centre, by which we live not from ourselves but from the gracious act of God. This is all true, but it is just here that the paradox comes: Paul tells his Christians at Corinth that the world is theirs—*now that they are Christians*! (3.22.) The Christian can now return into the world precisely because he has left it, because his relationship to it, his angle of approach has been decisively changed. Morality, moral excellence or the lack of it, does not consist in persons, places and things considered in themselves but the relation of the subject to them. Once a man is *in Christ* (1.4)—a magnificent, compendious and often-repeated phrase—these ordinary relations are profoundly modified. Sin places man as an object, depersonalized, on the periphery, like a particle of matter which is drawn by magnetic attraction into the orbit of another. The re-creation of man brought about by his incorporation by baptism into Christ places him once again at the epicentre, the mid-point of the world:

> All things are yours:
>   Whether Paul or Apollos or Cephas
>   Or the cosmos, or life, or death
>   Or the present or the future;
> All are yours
> And you are Christ's
> And Christ is God's. [3.22–3.]

The Christian is the measure of all things, the Christian as such, neither inferior nor superior, lay or cleric, but the Christian as he is in the Church is the standard, and his presence alone justifies apostolate, authority and indeed the whole of existence both spatial and temporal. Man, according to Scripture, is in the divine image and, despite the wound of his nature, still decisively orientated to God. "Beloved is man," goes one rabbinical saying, "for that he was created in the Image". The Church exists, therefore, for the perfecting of man.

"All things are yours"—the Christian cannot be indifferent to the destiny of the world. On the contrary, it is only through redeemed man that the universe can be fulfilled. The two destinies are interconnected, for man is the point at which nature transcends itself. The fact that this dictum, *panta hymon*, was used by philosophers of the Stoa and applied by them to the Just Man suggests that Paul is here conscripting the Stoic doctrine of the inner harmony between man, the *anima humana*, and the world, the *anima mundi*, in the service of a theology of terrestrial realities.

"And you are Christ's"—this is possible only in the Church. Just as man has to recapitulate the universe, so Christ recapitulates mankind. This is worked out in Paul's teaching of Christ as the new Adam, that is, the new man, in ch. 15 of this letter.

"And Christ is God's"—the world is redeemed through man, man is redeemed in and through Christ, his transformation coming about through what later Christian philosophers will call the Hypostatic Union. Paul would put it more simply by representing God as coming to us in Christ. Writing later to his Corinthian Christians he would say:

> God was reconciling the world to himself through Christ . . . and entrusting to us the reconciling word; we are therefore ambassadors for Christ, God making his appeal through us.[1]

This means that the world can return to God only through Christ. Therefore no-one can be saved except through some saving contact with Christ, which contact is effected in the Church; from which we can draw the further important deduction that the Church must be, ideally, commensurate with the whole of mankind, since it is certain that God wishes all to be saved. This means that Christianity, rather than being a religion, has rendered all religions obsolete. If

[1] It is from this passage that the familiar incarnational formula, much in use among Anglicans, is taken. It should, however, be stated that the expression "God was in Christ" is a mistranslation since it ignores both the periphrastic conjugation of the imperfect ("God was reconciling . . . ") and the Semitic use of the preposition "in", which we would here more naturally translate "through", "by means of".

the Buddhist, Muslim or Taoist is saved it will not be through Buddha or the Prophet or Confucius but through Christ.

This might lead us to consider a further problem, which can only be touched on here: Where are the boundaries of the Church? Where does the Church end and the world begin? Leaving aside the unreal dichotomy between a visible and invisible Church, the result of an unwholesome theological development in the Middle Ages, there are two problems here. There is the question of a hidden link with the Church binding those who are juridically beyond her frontiers; all admit the existence of such an economy of salvation, and yet the way in which it has been formulated has not always been helpful, especially when we think of the immense numbers involved—a world population multiplying with frightening rapidity precisely in those areas where the Church is barely represented and where as a result there is little chance, for most, of any sacramental contact. Another problem concerns the moral boundaries of the Church. The sinner, even the mortal sinner, does not cease on that account to be a member of the Church, but there will always be a dividing line within every Christian who is a sinner (and all are) between Church and world, and it will always be difficult to know where that line runs.

A final note of optimism. In Paul's words to the

Corinthian Church we are conscious of the assurance that, despite the apparent disproportion, the Church will always have the ascendancy over the world. This is expressed in many different ways in this letter; thus Paul states his conviction that the saints will judge the world (6.2), which means that they already share in some way in the lordship of the risen Christ over this age and this world-order, despite disparity in numbers and influence. This is the basis of the Christian's optimism in the face of the apparently impossible missionary task facing him. As Heinrich Schlier puts it: "God has made up his mind in favour of one new world, his new world in the Church; and therefore all the forms and structures of the world serve the purpose of carrying out his decision."[1] This conviction is the source of the Church's unfailing power of self-renewal and contemporaneity—which constitutes for "those who are without" such an insoluble riddle.

[1] In *Principalities and Powers*, London, Herder and Herder and Nelson (1961), p. 20.

I appeal to you, brethren, by the name of our
Lord Jesus Christ
That all of you agree
And that there be no dissensions among you
But that you be united in the same mind and
judgement.

Is Christ divided?

Do you not know that you are God's temple
And that God's spirit dwells in you?
If anyone destroys God's temple God will destroy
him
For God's temple is holy
And that temple you are.

Strive to excel in building up the Church.

2

CHURCH UNITY

THERE may, at first sight, seem little connection between what we have been discussing in the previous chapter and what the title of the present one conjures up in the mind. Despite the great numbers on the subscription rolls, Church unity remains a domestic concern and is played out within the frontiers of the different denominations. But we forget that the Church must be united not only for its own sake but for the sake of the witness which it is called upon to give in the world, and of the task which it is called upon to perform of fulfilling and perfecting the world and preparing it for the coming of the risen Lord. In reading 1 Corinthians, therefore, we shall have to bear in mind this wider context.

Though unity may be hard to define satisfactorily, we can say roughly that it has an outside and an inside; an outside in relation to the rest of reality, an inside in so far as it constitutes, in the definition of the *Oxford English Dictionary*, "an individual . . . formed of parts that constitute a whole; due interconnexion and coherence of parts". Loss of unity or identity in the case of any social organization, therefore, can come about either through its being absorbed into the environment, a process of assimilation to the patterns and laws of the surrounding medium, or through fragmentation from within, a break-up which destroys the inner cohesion of the whole. Either process is fatal, and both dangers faced the Christian community at Corinth in the early years of its existence and, indeed, down into the second century, to judge by the letter of Clement from Rome.

The problem of non-conformity and the preservation of the identity of the Church's life "on the outside" raised then, as it still does now, a whole host of practical difficulties for the practising Christian. And in case we think our difficulties in this so-called post-Christian age are unique, we should think of that small, disregarded and despised ghetto trying to live up to its call in the middle of a sophisticated and vicious city. Just as the ever-increasing segregation of Judaism and the theocratic Jewish state of the post-exilic period posed a multitude of practical problems—mixed marriages, dealings with people "outside the pale" like Samaritans, some of which became the problems of the early Christian Churches—so the hard fact of living in an intractable pagan milieu raised constant problems for the Corinthian Christian in his everyday existence: whether he could buy meat from the *makella*, the city butchers, since practically all of it had been sacrificed to idols; whether he could accept public office where he would have to go through preliminary religious ceremonies; whether he could have recourse to civil law courts in the case of an offence by a "brother" or "sister"; whether he had to continue living with a pagan partner who insulted the Faith—and so on. Every Christian living in a non-Christian environment, if he is part of the world at all, must find himself faced with these problems and with the danger of allowing himself to be "sucked in", absorbed, to imperceptibly drift into a "worldly" way of thinking and judging. We may be surprised, in reading on, to discover that some of our problems are not so different after all, though of course there are many which are: sending a child to a school which is non-Christian or only nominally Christian; difficulties of religious practice in certain types of employment; objection to the retention or use of nuclear weapons, and the like.

This problem of not conforming, keeping our Christian identity, has of course always been with the Church, both in regard to doctrine and morality. At the outset the difficulties were chiefly of the second kind; what Paul said to the community of Corinth—"not many of you are wise" (1.26)—would doubtless have applied to Christians anywhere in those early days. But with the conversion of philosophers, thinkers and men of culture the inevitable struggle on the part of the Church to realize her identity as a religion set in. This is the central problem of Church history in the second century, and how hard the process was we can deduce from the fact that there is hardly a single writer of that period whose works have survived whom we could entirely clear of suspect or definitely heretical statements in the light of the totality of Christian revelation. This would be true especially of the bold and sustained effort of Christian scholars of the Alexandrian school to state the meaning of the Gospel in terms of Greek religious thought.[1] In the wider contacts of Church and world the situation was fairly clear-cut in the first three centuries, the age of the great persecutions, and the Christians of later ages would look back with some nostalgia to the martyr-Church of the Catacombs when the issue was quite simply apostasy or death. With the Constantinian Peace the swing was in the opposite direction—the many conversions, a great number of which were no conversions at all, the rapid and universal introduction of infant baptism with the accompanying severance of the moment of incorporation and that of conversion, the presence of a large number who were only nominal mem-

[1] See, for a sympathetic treatment of this attempt, H. Rahner, *Greek Myths and Christian Mystery*, London (1963).

bers of the Church, the gradual identification in practice of the idea of the Church with a clerical caste in the service of both Church and State, culminating with the identification, in the Middle Ages, of the idea of the Church with that of ecumenical civilization itself. Now that we are in a process of disengagement, of a return to a condition in which the frontiers of Church and world are more clearly defined, the situation of the Corinthian community, in many ways similarly placed, should be of great interest to us.

The most obvious danger was that of a break-up "from the inside", of fragmentation and schism. The letter, in fact, begins with an exhortation to avoid "schisms" (1.10) and we learn later that the liturgical assembly (notice how the same word *ekklesia* is used here) is dogged by the same tendency to split up (11.18), a significant fact, since the liturgical gathering is the Church itself in its most characteristic expression. Now, at first blush, there might seem little we could learn for our own situation, in which "schism" is on a universal scale, concerning, that is, not just a local Church, the Church of, say, Milan, Paris or Chicago, but the mutual relations of worldwide Christian bodies. This, however, would be a short-sighted view, for Paul, in tracing division to its roots, lays bare for us too the sources of our divisions. We should note that he never allows his Christians to forget the living context of the

Great Church to which they belong. As Cerfaux puts it: "When speaking of the assembly of the Corinthians, Paul never loses sight of the totality of the Christian people, and all his statements have in mind either the Christian people or the Christian life as it is in principle, and this is by its very nature universal. Hence all his statements go to build up the idea of the unity of the whole Church, and go beyond the concrete situation to which they refer."[1] Thus, he reminds the Corinthians that his teaching and example are the same for them as for the other Churches (4.17) and enjoins that they abide by the customs obtaining in the generality of the communities founded by him—even on questions of some detail, such as the need for women to wear veils in the liturgical assembly (11.16) and to keep silence (14.34).

He insists straight away on the absolute necessity of unity. Schism is a sin because it forms a wilful obstacle to the plan of God, which is the result of his "secret and hidden wisdom" (2.7), aiming at nothing less than to bring forth a new regenerated humanity, unified through its attachment to the archetypal man. Since it is only the Church which can create out of the raw material of unredeemed, disgregate mankind this finished product, disunity within the Church directly thwarts the divine purpose. This is the "unity of

[1] *The Church in the Theology of St. Paul*, Herder (1959), p. 231.

faith", that is, unity *in* the Faith, which is the secret goal of history in the profound analysis of what Church unity means which we find in the encyclical letter to the Ephesians.[1]

But schism is not only a sin, it is a sacrilege. This is expressed by saying that they, the community at Corinth addressed collectively, not distributively, are a sacred temple which must have its Real Presence, the Spirit of God. This, therefore, is a social, not an individual, obligation and responsibility which is enjoined in solemn language: "If anyone destroy God's temple, God will destroy him." (3.16–17.) It is interesting to note here that the community is the temple but later, when warning them about what must have been the besetting temptation in that city renowned throughout the world for its brothels, he has to remind them that "your body is a temple of the Holy Spirit within you, which you have from God". (6.19.) The union of man and woman is a figure, a sign inhering in the divine intentionality, of the union of Christ with his Church, which gives to that union its value of Christian mystery or sacrament: "This is a great mystery, and I take it to mean Christ and the Church."[2]

[1] See especially Chapter 4.
[2] Eph. 5.32. *Sacramentum* is the usual translation for the Greek *mysterion*. This is the basic text for the Catholic view of marriage as sacrament. Anglicans prefer to speak here of a sacramental ministry.

The Church, then, is a community chosen out from a disparate humanity divided socially, politically and religiously. It must have a recognizable identity, it must be a unity. It is the one new race, the *tertium genus* of Tertullian, different from Jew and Hellene, the "new blood and spirit" of the second-century *Letter to Diognetus*.[1] In it all divisions are cancelled, since all are reborn to an absolutely new life; all barriers have to go down. This universal fellowship, much discussed in the world in Paul's century with the growing awareness of the meaning of the *oikoumene*, the one united world, preached by Stoic saints and itinerant Pythagorean missionaries, becomes suddenly a reality in the newly born Christian society. Paul could quote the Stoic poets Cleanthes and Aratus on the Hill of Mars in Athens,[2] to the effect that all mankind are children of God; he could even perhaps (though this is doubtful and disputed) take over an expression here and there from the liturgies of the mysteries at nearby Eleusis in which this consciousness of human equality is expressed. But within the Christian Church this flows as an unavoidable postulate from the very nature of the great act of God which

---

[1] In the *Letter to Diog.*, 1, the Christian Church is *Kainon touto genos*, "this new race". The threefold division into Jew, Hellene and Christian occurs often in early Christian literature.
[2] Acts 17.28.

is constitutive of the community; it is also complete and radical—"There is neither Jew nor Greek, there is neither slave nor free, there is neither male nor female; for you are all one in Christ Jesus."[1]

Thus it is no surprise to find the word most frequently used to describe this community is "fellowship", belonging together, but a special kind of belonging together. Christians belong together because they belong to Jesus Christ into whom they are baptized. (1.9.) And here we come to the root of the problem of unity for the Corinthians, since the letter was written in the first place to get them to understand that their baptism—for most of them a fairly recent event—and the accompanying instruction given by a Church leader did not involve an association with him or a particular and separatist loyalty, as might be the case with a philosophical school, a religious guild or something of the kind. Christian baptism was *into* Christ; it was a consecration to Christ involving the baptized in a unique association with him. We know in fact from the early Church that the original baptismal formula spoke of baptism in the name of the Lord Jesus. At the end of the First Gospel Christ commands his followers to baptize "in [into] the name of the Father, the Son and the Holy Spirit".[2] The Greek

[1] Gal. 3.28.
[2] Matt. 28.19.

3

use of the accusative "into" in this and similar expressions implies a dedication, a point we ought to bear in mind in making the Sign of the Cross, since this is in fact identical. This trinitarian form is found also in the *Didache*, an early-Church book, but is not witnessed in the apostolic period in the rest of the New Testament.

The conclusion is that the unity of the individual Christian with Christ, the *koinonia* (fellowship) brought about in baptism, is the foundation for the unity and fellowship between Christian and Christian, the cement of the fabric, to use a Pauline metaphor. That is why, in the opening words of greeting, Paul can speak of them having been called—at baptism—into fellowship (1.9).

We can perhaps try to go a little deeper here. The characteristic of Christian as opposed to any other initiation (for example, that of John the Baptist, still practised, as we have seen, in the early-Church period) was that it contained its own self-authentification in the giving of the Spirit, mostly in some external, ascertainable form. This was precisely the point at which the teaching of Apollos and the disciples of the Baptist had been defective. But the giving of the Spirit depended upon the single saving event of the death-resurrection-ascension of Jesus—"the Spirit had not yet been given because Jesus was not yet

glorified".[1] This also, incidentally, explains why
Luke has a strong strain of Elijah-typology in
the Ascension story, since the disciple of the
prophet could not receive his spirit until Elijah
was taken up and was *seen* to be taken up, and
the disciples of Jesus, too, strain their eyes to
watch him until he disappears from sight.[2]

There is therefore a clear parallel between the
action of the Spirit in the Pentecost of the Church
and in the Pentecost of each Christian which
occurs at baptism. The pouring out of the Spirit
is, in the Prophets, the principal sign of the in-
auguration of the messianic age, the "age to
come"—that is why Peter quotes a passage from
Joel about the last age in his first attempt to say
what had happened. The gift of charismatic,
ecstatic utterance given to the Apostles at Pentecost is paralleled in the same gift being bestowed
upon individual Christians at baptism (e.g., upon
Cornelius and his household). It is the evident
purpose of the Pentecost story to show that the
"age to come", the last age, the age of the Spirit,
is coextensive and identical with the age of the
Church. So the baptism of the Christian has to be
seen as a Pentecost to scale, the moment when the
individual enters into the charismatic *aion* of the
Church. There is also the strong undertone of

[1] John 7.39.
[2] See 2 Kings 2.10; Acts 1.10–11.

the unity of the whole human race, since we have reason to suspect that Luke, a deeply allusive writer, has in mind in the miraculous fact of mutual and simultaneous understanding among the nations the reversal of the disunity and mutual misunderstanding the origins of which are represented in the profound little story of the Tower of Babel. Paul's Christians at Corinth were evidently running the risk of losing sight of this basic and all-important implication of their baptism, and consequently breaking off into rival factions and splinter groups.

Thus it is no surprise that the different unitarian formulae that we find in Paul's letters are always connected with baptism. The best-known of these —"One Lord, one faith, one baptism"[1]—concentrates the whole idea of unity on the moment of baptism—the confession that is then made, "Jesus is the Lord", the faith that is then received, the whole rite which is symbolic of association with

[1] Eph. 4.5. Compare in the present-day rite, "What do you ask of the Church of God?" and the answer: "Faith." Other unitarian formulae in Paul: "One God ... and one Lord ... through whom we exist" (1 Cor. 8.6); "By one Spirit we were all baptized into one body —Jews or Greeks, slaves or free—and all were made to drink of one Spirit" (1 Cor. 12.13); "You are all one in Christ Jesus" (Gal. 3.28). The letters are full of similar phrases deriving from baptism. For the confession of faith, "Jesus is the Lord", see 12.3 and Rom. 10.9; Phil. 2.11.

the Lord at the moment of the great redemptive act.

It is therefore quite certainly New-Testament teaching that baptism is the basis of Church unity. It would, however, be possible for a person to be baptized and to profess allegiance to Jesus as Lord and yet to have received a defective prebaptismal instruction or *catechesis*. In the case of the disciples of John referred to above, who evidently considered themselves Christians of some sort, this instruction was so defective on a major point that they had to be rebaptized. I think we shall not be far wrong if we take this connection between baptism and baptismal instruction as the root of the trouble at Corinth and, indeed, among the Christian confessions today. For the baptismal instruction is nothing other than a summary of the spoken Gospel which begins from and ends in the risen Lord, and the baptismal confession of faith: "Jesus is the Lord" is nothing else than an act of faith in the reality of the Resurrection. It is this spoken word, the "good news of God" which went out from Jerusalem into the world from the day of Pentecost, which is passed on by the first "eye-witnesses and ministers of the word",[1] which no doubt Paul received in the house of Ananias at Damascus and which he in turn passed on, which constitutes tradition. With the mention of tradi-

[1] Luke 1.2.

tion we come to the burning centre of Church
unity and disunity both in the year 57 and 1964.

Here again, we shall have to content ourselves
with an outline within which we can read this
letter. The word, *paradosis* in Greek, means
literally a "handing-on". It can be used in an
active sense of the process of handing on or pas-
sively of the teachings which are handed on, what
the textbooks call *traditio passiva*. In the world
of the first century at Corinth the word might
have brought to the mind of the newly baptized
the handing on of secret teachings to the *mystes*
in the rites of Eleusis just a few miles away; for a
convert Jew it would at once remind him of the
traditions of the fathers, the teachings of the great
rabbis and rabbinical schools learnt by heart and
passed on word perfect from teacher to scholar,
from father to son.[1] Our Lord, we remember,
refers to these traditions in his disputes with the
Pharisees, the party specially tenacious of traditions, which, after the Fall of Jerusalem, gave its
character to Judaism which it has never completely lost. Paul himself tells us that he was,
before his conversion, "zealous for the traditions

[1] The Swedish scholar Harald Riesenfeld has attempted
to explain the fixity of the Gospel tradition with reference to the teachings of Jesus on the basis of the same
kind of transmission. See his paper read at the 1957
Oxford Congress in *The Gospels Reconsidered*, Black-
well (1960), pp. 131–53.

of the fathers". This gives us a clue as to how we should understand the word as in use in the early churches. It was essentially the Gospel, but the Gospel communicated orally and in its essential outline, not the whole written-up story as we have it now.

The best example of contemporary usage, illustrating what the word implied in both its aspects, can be found in ch. 15 of this letter, where Paul repeats and summarizes the Gospel which he himself had received and passed on. This proclaimed word takes us back six or seven years to the date of his first arrival in the city and, beyond this, to the day, thirteen or fourteen years earlier, when he himself had heard for the first time the saving word and, beyond this again, to the very first proclamation of the Good News. There is no break in the handing on: "I delivered to you as of first importance *what I also received* . . ." and there follows the Gospel in its essential lines: the death, burial and resurrection of Jesus. What Paul is at pains to stress, not just here but throughout, is that this traditional Gospel which each Christian receives at baptism must always remain the same, irrespective of who happens to be the agent of the handing on. "Whether then it was I or they [the Twelve], so we proclaim and so you have believed." (15.11.) It is this one unchangeable tradition which constitutes the Christian community as a unity confessing the same faith and which brings into existence in every age new Christian communities; in proportion as it is mutilated or corrupted Church unity must suffer. Paul tells his Christians that he brought them into existence *through* the Gospel (4.15); it is their duty to receive it and hand it on *as it is*, and only when through pride they forget this do factions appear: "What have you that you did not receive? If then you received it, why do you boast as if it were not a gift?" (4.7.) This is not just a vague exhortation to be humble; the word *receive* is used in the technical sense which associates it with the language which is mandatory when speaking of Church tradition. There is no room here for creativity; their greatest praise is to be faithful instruments of the creative act and gift of God.

One point where important divergencies had taken place was in the belief in the resurrection of the dead. This was a particularly hard bite to swallow for the dominant Gentile element in the community, since all their thinking had been made, consciously or not, within the reference scheme of anthropological dualism common to all Greek religious thinking. Salvation meant release not from sin but from the direct environment of the body, and here, just after getting rid of it, we are to get it back! What is interesting here is that this point is not explicit in the proclaimed Word, the *kerygma*, though it must have formed part of prebaptismal instruction or *cate-*

chesis; it is numbered among "elementary doctrines" by the writer of Hebrews.[1] Paul saw his
task as demonstrating the connection between
the credal facts and this theological conclusion;
he shows how the resurrection of the Christian
and the resurrection of Christ mutually inhere,
that the whole point of Christ's resurrection was
that it should be the prototype of ours, that he
rises as the firstfruits of the dead. Unity in the
faith, therefore, implies more than just belief that
Jesus rose from the dead.

Another example of a slightly different kind
will make this clearer, namely, the sacramental
life of the community. Different views on baptism
had been responsible for the existence of the four
factions mentioned at the beginning of the letter
(1.12), and the repetition and insistence on the
preservation of the early tradition on the
Eucharist provides a case which deserves special
consideration. At the beginning of this important
chapter Paul commends them for having kept the
traditions as he had handed them on to them
(11.2), but evidently there were some exceptions
and some misunderstandings. Hence, in the question of the assembly of the whole community
which normally would have ended with the celebration of the Eucharist, the necessity of repeating
(what they should already know as part of their

[1] Heb. 6.2.

instruction) what he had received from the Lord and delivered to them (11.23). Here the tradition is incorporated not in a fixed formula of words but in the living voice of the liturgical action. There were some who were no longer listening to that voice, who had introduced disorders of their own into the plenary assembly and taken from the *agape* of that Hellenistic world to which they belonged customs and practices which were having a disruptive influence. This can remind us of the important role played by the Liturgy in Church tradition; an example might be the old feast of the Dormition of the Virgin apropos the controversial dogma of the Assumption of Our Lady, a feast which witnessed indirectly to what was held in a certain part of the Church and in a certain period, in the absence of any other kind of documentation.

This absolute necessity of maintaining the tradition intact involves at once the question of authority in the Church. When concerned with discipline in the general assembly Paul makes his appeal to the practice of the "Churches of God". (11.16.)[1] This takes us a step further, since what he is doing here is, in effect, to insist on inter-church conformity in essentials of doctrine and

[1] An expression referring to the primitive Churches established in Jerusalem and Palestine, as can be seen by comparing it with "the Churches of Christ in Judaea" (Gal. 1.22; 1 Thess. 2.14; 2 Thess. 1.4).

liturgical practice, a uniformity which did not, of course, exclude variations. This appeal to the Jerusalem church as the spiritual centre (it still had a decade of life left) was not just in the matter of liturgical practice. The "Gospel" of Paul at Corinth was substantially identical with that of Peter in the early chapters of Acts, which was later to be written up and filled out for the benefit of the Roman Church in Mark's Gospel. The reason for this conformity, based on the conviction that Jesus had intended to found a universal church, not a federation, is not expounded in our letter. It finds expression in the way Luke planned his story in Acts, which traces the history of the New Israel, first centred on Jerusalem and ending in the journey to Rome.

The unity of the Christian body finds its perfect expression in what has always been considered as the sacrament of unity, the Eucharist. It is, in fact, called *communion* for the first time in our letter, and communion means not just union of the individual with Christ in the sacrament, but union with one another in the action which is being performed. Another designation which comes from the words of institution, "the New Covenant", has the same social implication, since a covenant or alliance must be made with one people, not an unco-ordinated mass or a mustering of dissident groups. It must therefore express a union *in actu*, not be used as a means of bringing such a union about, since all liturgy is an expression of life in society. One of the earliest and most widespread names for the eucharistic service", the Breaking of Bread", contains and expresses once again the idea of a united community.

> The bread which we break, is it not a participation in the body of Christ? Because there is one bread, we who are many are one body, for we all partake of the one bread. [10.16–17.]

The same idea is contained in the typological exegesis of the manna, one people sharing in one food (10.3–4); indeed, to read the early Fathers and the earliest liturgical forms, we might be led to think of this as the principal aspect of the Eucharist, namely, to express and intensify this idea of belonging to a divine society. This is brought out in the Roman liturgy of Hippolytus, from the beginning of the third century, in which the great Thanksgiving Prayer contains a petition that the Church be gathered together in unity, and the same petition is uppermost in the eucharistic service of the Didachist, which may well go back to the first century:

> As this broken bread was scattered over the hills and then, when gathered, became one mass, so may thy Church be gathered from the ends of the earth into thy kingdom.

Remember, O Lord, thy Church; deliver her from all evil, perfect her in thy love, and from the four winds assemble her, the sanctified, into thy kingdom which thou hast prepared for her.

It might seem a pity that we no longer use these prayers, since they express what we have for several centuries lost with the emergence of a silent, unintelligible liturgy, private stipended masses, and congregations which do not communicate, meals at which few or none eat. For Paul, as this letter shows, the eucharistic assembly or get-together is the *speculum* of the great, ingathered Church at the end of time, the point of maximum realization of the idea of the Church, the supreme means of bringing within the scope of common experience that sense of mysterious solidarity and corporate personality which the Christian idea implies. That is why all discussions on Church unity—between Catholics and Protestants, Anglicans and Methodists, East and West —always pivot on the Eucharist.[1]

It was with special reference to disorders in the weekly assembly that Paul tried to break in

[1] The Eucharist as the sacrament of unity is accepted on principle. This is emphasized in the Methodist statement on the sacraments in the recent conversations with the Church of England. See the *Report on the Conversations* (1963), p. 32. In the Order for the Church of South India Paul's saying about all being one bread comes at the beginning.

these people, naturally rather refractory and quarrelsome, to the social qualities which have to be developed if the sense of community is to be acquired. He appeals to them to get into the habit of thinking together and being prepared to give up some of their autonomy for the common good. (4.6,18.) This went against the general climate of extreme individualism which the old Greek *polis* had fostered and which still remained an ideal. Some idea of the difference between the Christian *ekklesia* and that of the average Greek city can be had by reading how one such assembly, of Ephesus in this case, was likely to end up.[1]

In casting around for compelling images to express this all-important unity, Paul makes use of anything he can find which would serve. This task was probably made easier by the Stoic concept of the whole world as a unity or organism held together from the centre. In fact the author of the Alexandrian Book of Wisdom had, about a century earlier and in an idiom with which Paul must have been familiar since he certainly knew this work, expressed a truth about Wisdom in Stoic terminology; the couplet is well known from the liturgy of Pentecost:

The spirit of the Lord has filled the universe,
And that which holds together all has knowledge
   of [every] voice. [Wisd. of Sol. 1.7.]

[1] Acts 19.23–20.1.

Elsewhere, when he is speaking of the "diversity of gifts" which they had received, he finds, since it is a question of function, the metaphor of the different members of the one body useful. (12.12–27.) This was quite commonly used in the contemporary world and probably goes back to the well-known fable of Aesop. Each one has to bring his contribution to the life of the body—exposition of Scripture, ecstatic prayer, prophecy, miracles, teaching and the rest; they not only make up one body but they *are* "the body of Christ". (12.27.) More frequently, in this letter at least, he speaks of the Corinthian community as a building which could be destroyed, pulled down by schism. The foundation is the Gospel, the proclaimed Word of God (2.10–16), to which the superstructure must correspond if it is to last. This temple is built for the Spirit, the divine indweller of the Church. This simply develops and applies the passages in which the Old Testament speaks of Israel as the House of God.

It is on the basis of a reading of this letter carried through with an eye on the points mentioned above that we can best assess the extent of our existing unity and what remains to be done. We are baptized, we have received the Spirit, we are therefore in saving contact with the great redemptive act. We believe that Jesus is the Lord and accept the oral Gospel as Paul summarizes it in ch. 15. We still, however, disagree on some conclusions, both for doctrine and for morals, which are drawn from this Gospel and, most of all, on the nature of the universal society which Christ founded. It is only when we assess fully and accept with gratitude but without complacency the degree of unity already there that we should go on to discuss the remaining difficulties with charity and mutual sympathy.

This is how one should regard us
As servants of Christ and stewards of the mysteries
    of God
Moreover, it is required of stewards that they be
    found faithful.

Make love your aim

There are varieties of gifts but the same Spirit
And there are varieties of service but the same
    Lord
And there are varieties of functions, but it is the
    same God
Who inspires them all in every one.

To the weak I became weak that I might win
    the weak
I have become all things to all men
That I might by all means save some.

AUTHORITY AND HIERARCHY

ONE of the difficulties which Catholics often meet in discussion with other Christians is that for many of the latter the Catholic Church seems to project an image of a solid, monolithic and almost totalitarian system which leaves its members little freedom of movement and hardly enough room to breathe. For Catholics themselves, those who are not content to play the role of obedient but passive sheep, the presence of authority and the insistence on obedience are sometimes painfully obvious. Often enough authority, and obedience, which is so closely linked to it (the *Oxford English Dictionary* defines authority as "the power to enforce obedience") are accepted with resignation, with a shrug of the shoulders, as being necessary for life in society—society of any kind—and therefore for life in the Church. But with an admission of this kind we can easily, if we are not careful, assimilate the Church to the pattern of secular societies and in particular the State—which, whatever else we may say about it, is not what emerges from a reading of this letter.

At the centre of the life of the Church is the mystery of the encounter between God and man and the divine life which is communicated through that encounter. Everything subserves this mystery because it is this alone which counts in the last analysis. And since this saving encounter is made possible to man as member of a community, organization, hierarchy and jurisdiction are necessary—but they, too, come under the Mystery. To dichotomize Church as society and Church as mystery is therefore false and misleading. This was made clear in *Mystici Corporis*:

> We therefore deplore and condemn also the calamitous error which invents an imaginary Church, a society nurtured and shaped by charity, with which it disparagingly contrasts another society which it calls juridical. Those who make this totally erroneous distinction fail to understand that it was one and the same purpose—namely, that of perpetuating on this earth the salutary work of the Redemption—which caused the divine Redeemer both to give the community of human beings founded by Him the constitution of a society . . . and also to have it enriched by the Holy Spirit with heavenly gifts and powers.[1]

To say this, of course, removes neither the practical difficulties in the way of understanding what

[1] C.T.S. translation, para. 63.

authority in the Church really means nor the need for constant self-examination and vigilance in the uses to which authority is put.

In the secular world the sources of authority lie near the sources of power. It is man who has dominion, man who shapes the world by his brain and brawn to ends selected by himself. What may surprise us, is to find that the Scriptures not only frankly accept this fact but even radicalize man's power and authority in the world. "Now in putting everything in subjection to man," writes one New-Testament theologian, "he [God] has left nothing outside his control."[1] This follows a quotation from the magnificent poem to Man in Psalm 8, and this in its turn takes us back to the story of creation and the command given to man to subdue the earth and have dominion, for "the heaven is the Lord's; but the earth he has given to the sons of men".[2] This has to be recognized as a scriptural datum. The object of the Church's presence in the world is not to question or deny this, much less to maim life, but to give it and give it more abundantly. No view of the Church's function in human society will ever be felt to be adequate or permit its members to give their witness in the centre of life if man's need to actualize his tremendous potential is not acknowledged.

[1] Heb. 2.8.
[2] Ps. 115.28.

But at the same time the Scriptures speak to us of man's wound. What the early chapters of Genesis tell us is that the constant attempt at self-fulfilment and autonomous existence reveals in man, as his history unfolds, a radical disability. This movement to autonomy, undertaken with such confidence but outside the divine will, succeeds by a baffling paradox only in increasing the area of disorder and death until we come to the point of total, or almost total, annihilation in the Flood. Paul had certainly meditated long on this radical disability both in Gentile and Jew— the failure to reach authentic existence. He speaks of it often, and writing to the Philippians he takes occasion from an exhortation to humility to speak of the failure of natural man (Adam) and the new way to fulfilment opened up by the new man (Christ):

Have this mind among yourselves, which you have in Christ Jesus, who, though he was in the form of God did not [like Adam] count equality with God a thing to be grasped, but emptied himself, taking the form of a servant . . . he became obedient unto death, even death on a cross. [2.5–8.]

This at once indicates the level at which we are to think of obedience and authority as practised in the Church.

To return to our letter. "There are varieties of

ministries but the same Lord." (12.5.) In practice
authority takes many forms but, in fact, for the
Christian in the Church, belongs only to the
Lord, the *Kyrios*, the risen Christ. This authority
is his because given to him—"All authority is
given to me"[1]—and the apostolic mission follows
from this, as can be seen from the "therefore"
—"Going, therefore, make disciples of all
nations . . ."—a mission which, though addressed
to the Eleven, is in fact shared by all Christians;
any Christian can baptize.

It should be noted straight away that the word
which we translate "authority" in this text—
exousia—is not used in the New Testament of
apostles and Church leaders, for, as Paul states
elsewhere, "There is no *exousia except from*
God",[2] and the word was already too much
associated with secular power, that of the State
and its ruler. We are therefore free to conclude
at once that there is no parity as between the
exercise of authority in the Church and in the
secular sphere, a conclusion already present in
the Gospel sayings about the first being the least
and the leader being as a servant; the Lord, in
fact, speaks of the rulers and great men of the
world exercising authority and lording it over
their subjects—"but it shall not be so among

[1] Matt. 28.18.
[2] Rom. 13.1.

you".[1] Authority is exclusive to God, a fact that the Scriptures represent under the metaphor of the divine kingship. This authority is entrusted to the risen Lord, a fact decisive for Paul's interpretation of history. He will subject all other "authorities" to himself and then the kingdom will return to the Father and the cycle will be complete. (15.20–28.)

It follows that the exercise of authority must always depend on a divine call and be in function of the divine dispensation. The standard term used for those who have this responsibility is *diakonos*, "minister"—a term borrowed from economic life and meaning a waiter, attendant or servant of some kind. Thus there is the service (*diakonia*) of the Word to which the Apostles have to give themselves, the service of the Church, the service of the "saints" to which Stephanas and his colleagues in Corinth had so generously given their time and energies. (16.15.) It is only later on that the term *diakonos* is restricted to a definite Church order with a fixed status, composed of men and women associated with the bishop or president in the management of the local Church.[2]

[1] Matt. 20.26.
[2] For these terms see Acts 6.3; Col. 1.25. Deacons begin to be mentioned regularly in the Pastorals and early sub-apostolic writings, e.g., 1 Tim. 3.8ff; 1 Clement 42.4. Deaconesses are referred to in 1 Tim. 3.11. Only Phoebe (Rom. 16.1) is known for certain by name, but

Paul uses other terms for Church leadership here and there in this letter. He describes Sosthenes and himself as "co-workers" with God (3.9) and as "ministers" and "stewards of God's mysteries". This word "minister" (*hyperetes*), which could mean anything from a bricklayer's mate to a synagogue attendant, usually has the same Christian significance as *diakonos* in the New Testament. Thus Luke calls the first-generation Christian missionaries "ministers of the Word". The *diakonos* or *hyperetes* has to be totally at the service of the Church and fully aware that he holds the position which he does only in virtue of something greater than himself. He has no other purpose than to create the circumstances propitious for God to act—nothing else. "What then is Apollos, what is Paul? *Ministers* through whom you came to believe..." (3.45); Paul planted by his catechizing, Apollos came along from Ephesus and watered the seed which had been planted, but the vital immanent operation, to do with the personal life of each in Christ, the increase, could come only from God. Everything in the Church is at the service of this central, mysterious creative operation.

It can never be sufficiently pondered by Christians, especially those "in authority", that their

---

some of the other women who come in for praise in the letters must surely have belonged to this class.

fundamental equality flows from the fact of their baptism "into one body", that of Christ, and their consequent endowment with his spirit (12.13). Nothing can change that. Christians of the first hour expressed this in the beautiful appellation of "Brother" and "Sister" given to one another. God moves each one to contribute his or her share to the task of "edification", building up the unity and perfection of the whole body. Paul expresses this in a trinitarian formula:

There are varieties of gifts—but the same Spirit
There are varieties of service—but the same Lord
There are varieties of function—but the same
    God. [12.4–6.]

All that is in the Church and makes the Church what it is comes from the one source—the divine life of the Trinity. The manifestations of the Spirit in the charismatic gifts, of the lordship and authority of the risen Lord in the Church's hierarchical *diakonia*, of the various activities carried out—all these only make sense when referred to the source from which they come and the purpose they serve in the Church. The end of every kind of activity is, to use a typical Pauline word, edification. The edge has been very much taken off this word, so that it no longer has the strong biblical sense it once had, rooted in its semantic origin. Where the Douai version reports Paul's exhortation, "Seek to abound unto the edifying

of the church" (14.12), we should rather think
of his original figure of the Church as a sacred
building, a temple or sanctuary, work on which
has to be continued until the last brick is in place.
He calls his Christians at Corinth "God's plot
and God's building" (3.9), both traditional Old-
Testament metaphors for the Chosen People. The
former is developed in the image of the vineyard
and olive tree,[1] the latter is worked pretty
thoroughly in the letter we are discussing.

There is one aspect of the Christian life of those
early days which we may find rather baffling;
what are called in this letter *charismata*, or free
gifts—spontaneous outpourings of spiritual energy
such as ecstatic prayer or the gift of healing. The
question at once arises here whether we should
always feel ourselves obliged nowadays to put
the same interpretation on these as did the Corinthians, and the ground was no doubt prepared not
only by the temperament of these rather volatile
Levantines, but also, in particular, by their prior
acquaintance at close hand with the Dionysiac
cult, with its ecstatic and mantic characteristics.
Paul, therefore, continually insists that, whatever
one may say of the inspirational origin of these
phenomena, they must always contribute to the
common good and not become, as they easily
could, a solvent of unity. Here, however, we are

[1] Especially in Rom. 11.17–24.

not concerned with questions of psychology or parapsychology, interesting though they may be, but with these "manifestations of the Spirit" (12.7) in so far as they bring us up against a point of crucial importance for our understanding of the nature of ecclesiastical authority and its relation to hierarchy. Do these represent a stage of charismatic government of the community which was displaced in the course of historical development in favour of a juridical society divided up into governors and governed? And does this change signify the end of the primitive Church and the beginning of the Catholic Church, with the undesirable characteristics referred to above?[1]

[1] In view of the interesting parallels which have been pointed out between the organization of the Qumran sectarian "religious" and the primitive Jerusalem Church, the prototype and ideal for the others, it ought to be noted that in the community rule of the former we find, side by side with an exalted theology of the community, a very clear and sharply differentiated hierarchical system, a strong sense of order and jurisdiction and a well-defined distinction between clergy and laity. The *mebakker* had roughly the same functions as the bishop came to have (the two words mean the same, in fact), the governing body was composed of three priests and twelve (or, less probably, nine) laymen, and the sacred community was known as The Many (*rabbim*), as we find in the New Testament. Interesting for our theme is how the organization of the assembly as a whole is exactly reflected in the rules for the sacred meal, which was both the *speculum* of the whole body

We can go some way to answering this question by taking simple note of what these special gifts were—not all were of the ecstatic or abnormal kind—and drawing one or two conclusions from the way in which they are presented. We find four lists in Paul's letters:

Rom. 12.6ff.	*Eph. 4.11*	*1 Cor. 12.8ff.*	*1 Cor. 12.28ff.*
Prophecy	Apostolate	Exposition	Apostolate
Ministry	Prophecy	Knowledge	Prophecy
Teaching	Evangelising	Faith	Teaching
Exhortation	Pastoral	Healing	Miracles
Almoner	Teaching	Miracles	Healing
Presiding		Prophecy	Assistance
Acts of Mercy		Discernment	Direction
		Tongues	Tongues
		Interpretation	

Now, what strikes us at once about these lists is the great diversification of function within the

---

and its concrete realization. The Qumran Covenanters conceived of their community as the result of an eternal plan or design; they used terms such as "The Way", "The Saints", "The Covenant of God" and "The Sons of Light" of themselves, all of which can be paralleled in the New Testament. It was very definitely a more juridical and less charismatic group than the early Church, with severe and precise penalties for infringement of rules—e.g., for lying about the value of property handed over to the community. (Cf. Acts 5.) It also enforced a compulsory retiring age, fixed at sixty, since "God has ordained that their understanding should depart even before their days are complete".

Church which they show; and we must not forget that they were not created by appointment from above or by any system of allocation, but from the person himself, who was conscious of being moved by the Spirit to contribute to the community in one or other of these ways. Not all are now easy to explain; "apostle" and "evangelist" evidently do not have the sense they now have for us, and the gift of tongues would need a chapter, indeed a book, all to itself. What we can see at a glance is that there could have been no hard-and-fast distinction between charismatic and juridical functions; consequently, the whole idea of a charismatic Church succeeded by a jurisdictional Church is based on an unreal dichotomy, a conclusion to which recent studies on early-Church offices also point. What is for our purposes significant is that many of these gifts have come to be exercised within Church orders. This is true at least of ministry (*diakonia*), teaching, of the evangelist and the pastor, and probably of other instances also. Here again we are led to the conclusion, without going into the complicated process by which Church orders evolved and crystallized, that these early Christians did not think in terms of authority over against the operations of the Spirit. The exercise of pastoral ministry, the office of teacher, instructor and exhorter, the organization of the Church on the economical and financial level (for these questions also arose then as now), the management of public assemblies—all are seen as coming from the operation of the Spirit and in virtue of the unity and growth of the whole body. Church leadership and charismatic endowment were not considered as mutually exclusive; indeed, it could well happen that the two coincided, as was the case with the Church of Antioch.[1] Paul himself, on more than one occasion, supported his claim to the status of an apostle (this had been denied also at Corinth) with reminders of his ecstatic experiences. Any kind of office in the Church, therefore, had to be charismatic, though not necessarily in the sense of the possession of extraordinary gifts such as those of ecstatic utterance or prophecy.

Perhaps we can clarify this point by distinguishing between charismatic grace and grace of state, though this latter is a relatively modern term, and while suitable enough as a descriptive label is often subject in practice to misunderstanding, especially in the absence of a sound and accepted biblical theology of Church office and authority. If we place it in the category of grace we must remember that it is a *gratia sufficiens*, not a *gratia efficax*, that is, it has to be co-operated with, as is perfectly clear from what Paul says in this letter to the effect that the grace of the apostolate could have been made void in him if he had not "worked

[1] See Acts 13.1.

harder than any of them". (15.10.) It does not automatically endow its beneficiary with personal infallibility or, much less, impeccability; it is, on the contrary, an opportunity to serve others, to co-operate in building up the body of Christ. At least, that is how it emerges from a reading of this letter. It is interesting that in the list of charismatic offices which are the object of ambition (12.29–30) the only ones missing of the lists we have just seen are those of government or direction and assistance!

All this gives us an insight into how the whole question of organization and government was viewed before the period of consolidation represented by the Pastoral Epistles set in. There is, first of all, the apostolate in the strict primitive sense, the claim of which is absolute on account of the authentication it possesses through witness to the risen Christ. Paul never conceded anything here, as one can see through the directly polemic, almost harsh, note which he sounds straight away in his letter to the Galatian Christians. Next we can see from the four lists that there existed in each Church the office of "government" or direction with "assistants", which would correspond to the bishops and deacons mentioned more than once in the later letters (e.g., Phil. 1.1), but the important tasks of teaching, catechizing, almsgiving, financial administration, collecting for the needy Christians of Jerusalem and the like, were spread over a wide area. Not all would have been performed by the deacon, even at a much later stage of development than this. In the "pastors" of the Ephesians list we may well have, as Père Allo puts it, the makings of what later became the local clergy entrusted, as the name suggests, with pastoral duties.[1] We know, incidentally, from the *Didache* (ch. 15) that these Church offices required the laying on of hands, what we now call ordination, and that candidates could be and were elected sometimes by the people—a practice which was continued for centuries. We also learn from the same source that the strictly charismatic offices (for example, prophecy) were held in greater honour than those of Church administration.

It would be only at the risk of leaving ourselves open to the charge of excessive ingenuousness if we were to speak of going back behind all the formidable canonical and juridical developments of the Church's long history to an idyllic primitive stage of blessed freedom from tiresome canonical regulations and exigent bishops and their representatives. At the same time, when we speak of the *power* of order and the *power* of jurisdiction invested in the Hierarchy (for that is the classical formulation of canonists and theologians), we must take care to examine our formulae in the

---

[1] *Première Epître aux Corinthiens*, 2nd ed., Paris (1956), p. 337.

4

light of biblical truth and remember that, theo-
logically, hierarchy in the Church is in the same
order of reality as the Incarnation itself, that of
mediation. Just as the human nature of Christ is
the instrument of the action of God on mankind,
so must the Church, so long as mankind lasts,
provide the means for that action to make contact
with men—which involves a continuation of the
same kind of mediation. The Hierarchy is therefore the vehicle of the divine *dynamis* passed on
through the glorified Lord at the right hand of the
Father. St Thomas puts it in this way, that God has
decided to give men not only the perfection by
which he exists but also his own *virtus causativa*,
the ability to co-operate in producing that life in
others. In this sense, according to St Thomas'
teaching, the Hierarchy can be considered an
instrumental cause of the Church. Our Lord himself said that the believer in him would do even
greater things than he did "because I go to the
Father"; it is therefore the presence of the Lord
at the right hand of the Power which accounts
for the life of the Church in all its manifestations.

We pass on now to one or two practical con-
siderations which should touch on our own contemporary problems in this regard. Paul was no
Rousseau, much less a long-haired anarchist. He
saw order built into nature, something in the way
that Shakespeare did, as for example in the well-
known Ulysses speech in *Troilus and Cressida*.

And if nature requires order, order requires and indeed presupposes hierarchy in the most general sense of the word. One type of hierarchy, a fundamental one, is brought in quite casually in discussing the regulation of the weekly meeting. He asks the women to keep the rules and customs of this assembly on the grounds of an order which springs from nature: God—Christ—man—woman. (11.3.) Paul the rabbi deduces this order also from the Scriptures by exegetical arguments which might seem to us today, admittedly, somewhat *recherchés*. If we look at the four lists above we can deduce a rudimentary hierarchy of a different kind, since some of the gifts are of greater value and relevance to Church life than others, though all must serve the purpose of Church unity, of the proclamation of the word of God which builds up the Church. All, too, must be exercised within the love—*agape*, Paul calls it—which signifies the bond of union within the community. The well-known chapter in praise of love (13) will be very largely misinterpreted if we think only of love of one person for another, in whatever way we construe it. It is first and foremost a gift, the greatest of the gifts which spring from Christian fellowship, which unites each one to the brotherhood in spite of the centripetal tendencies of his or her selfhood. The other charismatic gifts *and* Church offices are subject to this love to the extent that if they are exercised outside it they are nothing—

an empty shell—and the voice of authority nothing but a noisy gong or a clanging cymbal. "Make love your aim" (14.1) is addressed not only to the ecstatics and prophets, but to all concerned in Church government and leadership.

Can a study of this letter throw any light on the concrete difficulties felt by thoughtful Catholics in this area today? There are quite a number of problems which worry us which Paul dealt with in speaking to other communities and some which he did not deal with at all, but at least a basis for discussion can be set up with special reference to three questions which are still relevant.

First: The most obvious and striking organizational feature in the Catholic church today is the division between clergy and laity as two classes, sometimes separated by quite a high wall! Hence arises the question of lay status as a special problem in its own right, nowadays so much discussed, though sometimes with more vehemence than clarity. A lay theology has become a necessity and a priority precisely because of the decline in corporate sense and in the realization of what Church membership means at a level which can contemplate the fundamental equality of all who have been baptized and received the Spirit. In practice, of course, this realization—which is uppermost in this letter—requires much co-operation and give-and-take if it is going to have its effect.

A consideration of the charismatic and prophetic function in the Church would go a long way to dispelling the idea of a division into first- and second-class citizen status. The usual approach, as we have seen, has been that these functions went out fairly early, about the time of Irenaeus, having been intended only for the "edification" of the nascent community. All religious movements, it is argued, go through this period of "enthusiasm"—George Fox and the Friends, Joseph Smith and the Mormons, for example. The Christian Church, *quâ* religious movement, had its charismatic period which served its purpose and came to an end. In any case, it is argued further, in the light of our greatly increased knowledge of psychosomatic disturbances, we might not always be able to take the same view of these phenomena as Paul and his contemporaries did. The answer to this is that these phenomena have never disappeared from the history of the Church because they were never intended to. The charismatic function—understood in its widest sense as we have seen it in the lists—and the prophetic function are necessary for the health of the organism. If the lives of the saints—both lay and clerical—mean anything at all, once the necessary subtractions have been made, they show at least surely this, that the Spirit has not been quenched. The career of Catherine of Siena is one of a score of examples which come to mind. The convening of a general council of the Church was ascribed by John XXIII to a charismatic impulse, and the setting on foot of so many lay movements in the modern epoch must have something of the same kind at their origin. *All* Christians have received the Spirit at baptism.

Second: Intimately connected with the first point is the gradual centralization and telescoping of functions in the Church. Leaving out the purely charismatic offices, the four lists contain, as we have seen, a good number of presumably permanent offices which cover very many aspects of the external life of the Christian community evenly spread out. Most of these, as we have also seen, have been absorbed into functions of holy orders, the reception of which is preceded by tonsure as a ceremony of initiation into the clerical state. The four minor orders play only a small part in the life of the Church, namely, to punctuate the progress of the clerical student to major orders and the priesthood, while the subdiaconate is exclusively liturgical in character. Two approaches to a solution of the difficulties caused by this undue centralization of functions might be mentioned: to revitalize the ancient office of the diaconate as a permanent status, held by men either married or single, who would be able to play a considerable part in the life of the parish both liturgically and in administration; and to show a greater willingness to spread over a wider area the functions and responsibilities implied in the four lists—especially in the case of economic and financial administration.[1] This would also have the excellent advantage of releasing many Church leaders from chores, even important ones, which can be done by others, thus leaving them much freer for the essential *cura pastoralis*, and more accessible to their flock.

What, however, often provides a much more pressing problem—and this is our third and final point—is not so much the theory but the practice of authority in the Church. Paul's example in this letter is very precious in this regard. It is wonderful to read how words of sarcasm change imperceptibly into words of touching reproach and affection—" . . . I am not writing this to make you ashamed but to admonish you as my beloved children. For though you have countless guides in Christ, you do not have many fathers". (4.8ff.) The *pater abbas* is never lost sight of in the administrator or the business man, as can so easily happen. He does not shelter behind a mystique of authority, secure in the armour-plating of divine sanctions. He is open, he lets himself be known, he is willing to defend himself against charges. He is in constant touch with them, letting them know how things are with him in Ephesus, what he is suffering (4.8ff)—this especially in the

[1] The second session of the Council has already made decisive strides in this direction.

wonderful autobiographical passage in 2 Cor. 12.1–12, at the end of which he pulls himself up, ashamed of himself—"I have been a fool, but you forced me to it!"[1] He does not have the habit of relying on their ignorance of their rights and privileges to "put the screw on"—on the contrary, he insists, to what seems at times an almost painful degree, on their liberty as Christians— to such an extent, indeed, that his saying, "All things are lawful" (6.12; 10.23), often repeated and taken out of its context, became an occasion of misunderstanding and abuse. He had to an eminent degree the quality of spiritual paternity, which meant that he could quite un-selfconsciously propose himself as an example to be imitated by those in his charge—a thing which it is normally difficult to do without causing either ribald mirth or at least mild sarcasm. "Be imitators of me as I am of Christ" (11.1)—not the first part without the second! "I am sending Timothy to you . . . to remind you of my conduct *in Christ* . . . " (4.17). This, when we come to think of it, implied, on the human level, a very high degree of openness and sincerity, and Paul's sincerity is always evident, sometimes painfully and embarrassingly so.

This did not mean that he eschewed plain speaking when the occasion arose. "The kingdom

[1] 2 Cor. 12.11.

of God does not consist in talk but in power"
(4.20) he curtly reminded them. "What do you
want? Shall I come to you with a rod or with
love in a spirit of gentleness?" (4.21.) We notice,
however, that the imperative mood is not over-
worked in this letter; only in isolated cases does
he lay down the law—in the case of binding traditions (2.17), for the collection in aid of the poor
of the mother-Church—a work which he had
always at heart and which is very significant for
the idea of Church unity (16.1)—very little else.
He also believes evidently in giving reasons for
any orders he gives. There is no such thing as
blind obedience for Paul—he wants them to obey
with their eyes wide open. Thus, in telling them
to avoid pagan sacrificial meals (our *communicatio
in sacris*), he begins: "I am speaking as to sensible
men; judge for yourselves"—just a suggestion of
"playing up" perhaps, but this in fact preludes a
magnificent exposition of the implications of such
an act if performed knowingly. There is the same
invitation to weigh for themselves the evidence he
places before them in dissuading women from
going bareheaded in the weekly assembly (11.13);
if they still find difficulty in obeying he appeals to
the traditions and customs as everywhere observed
among the Churches, in particular in "the Churches
of God", for him the final appeal, and leaves
it at that.

This penetration of Paul's mind on the question

of authority is a fascinating and rewarding task. Thus, we have referred already to the consciousness of an infallible charism in Paul as flowing from his sense of the apostolate. But he does not see this as a personal charism, something *there* at his disposal under all circumstances. This can be seen in the way in which he gives orders. In deciding what state of life is best (in answer to a specific question) he only *wishes* that they be as he is (7.7) whereas, in the matter of the prohibition of divorce, he says, "I command, not I but the Lord". (7.10.) This corresponds to a sedulous distinction between what comes from him personally and what comes from the living and infallible tradition of the Church: "Not I but the Lord", "Not the Lord but I." The root of infallibility is Jesus present in the Church and in the living Gospel tradition which the Church exists to defend. The Apostles enjoy this prerogative only on account of their having experienced this presence in a special way and only for the preservation of the Gospel. That is why Paul can say in another letter: "Even if an angel from heaven should preach a gospel to you besides that which we have preached to you, let him be accursed!" (Gal. 1.8); that is also why, in speaking to the Corinthians, he can make the astounding claim that he has the mind of Christ (2.16), and indeed show it in practice as in the excommunication of the incestuous Christian (5.1–5).

The great temptation is always to forget that authority is received and is not given to be an end in itself, *propter se*. Before concluding what is our second canonical letter, in preparation for his imminent visit, he writes: "I write this while I am away from you, in order that when I come I may not have to be severe in my use of the authority which the Lord has given me *for building up and not for tearing down*." (2 Cor. 13.10.) Paul knew only too well how the abuse of authority can in fact tear down, deform, stunt and dissipate the enormous energies for good in every person. This is true of the exercise of authority in any context, for example, that of parental authority. It is always instructive to go to the end of Paul's letters (a better word might be "addresses", since they were read out loud in the assembly of Christians, many of whom would not have been able to read) and look at the special word spoken to particular groups; thus at the end of Ephesians a word to the children, who were sitting perhaps cross-legged in front of their elders, in specially simple language for them to understand:

Children, obey your parents in the Lord, for that is the right thing to do. "Honour your father and mother"—this is the first commandment, and a promise goes with it.[1]

[1] Eph. 6.1–2.

This is followed by an admonition addressed to parents warning them not to provoke their children to anger. Elsewhere he warns against the particularly insidious danger of reverential fear, telling them not to *work on* their children in such a way as to make them timid and lacking in the necessary self-confidence to face the world.[1] All of this makes us see more clearly the mind of this great and generous man.

There are many other aspects of that mind which could be discussed: his adaptability—"all things to all men" (9.22); becoming weak with the weak (not strong with the weak and weak with the strong, a recurrent temptation!); his readiness to waive his rights, leading him to work day and night for his living rather than burden others —"I would rather die than let anyone deprive me of my grounds for boasting!" he says, half in jest (9.15). The exercise of authority in any circumstances, but especially in the institutional life of the Church, can only remain Christian by being true to that pattern.

[1] Col. 3.21.

By one Spirit we were all baptized into one body
Jews or Greeks, slaves or free—
And all were made to drink of one Spirit

He is the source of your life in Christ Jesus

The cup of blessing which we bless
Is it not a participation in the blood of Christ?
The bread which we break
Is it not a participation in the body of Christ?
Because there is one bread
We the Many are one body.

As often as you eat this bread and drink the cup
You proclaim the Lord's death until he comes.

SACRAMENTAL LIFE IN THE CHURCH

I T WILL seem at first sight straining things rather too far to try to compare what sacramental life in the Church means for us today with what it meant for a Christian community living in the fifth decade of the first century. For us the pattern is long familiar, perhaps too familiar—we realize the sacraments, the list of which we have learnt in the Catechism, are somehow very important for our life as Christians, and so we get our children baptized, we go to confession, go to Communion, get married "inside the Church", fetch a priest when anyone is dying, because all this is our duty as good Catholics. We do not contemplate any other pattern or order. The Christians to whom Paul addressed this letter, however, had no such pattern. They did not bring their children to church to be baptized a few days after birth and no bishop went round confirming the seven-year-olds. They could not drop in to confession on their way home from work and their eucharistic assembly, held in the private house of Stephanas or some other prominent "brother", at which they held the Bread in their hands and passed round the Cup, would very possibly have remained undetected for what it was by a present-day Christian if, by some time-machine journey through the past, he could have witnessed it. None of the sacraments, in fact, is mentioned apart from baptism and the Eucharist, nor does the word itself appear.

This suggests that it might be better for us, in our effort to rethink our sacramental life in the Church, to change tactics and begin this time at our end, working back from our situation to that which obtained in the first century with the hope that in the process we may begin to understand better the essential structure, the underlying realities, which are so often buried by custom and routine. For we must admit that there is no difference in the essential life in Christ whether lived in the first or the twentieth century, despite what may appear from a superficial examination. A comparison, therefore, should be a useful tool for the task of penetration below the surface; for we are by now agreed that this kind of penetration is absolutely necessary if we are to do what is necessary on our part in terms of theology both pure and applied towards a united Christendom.

To start with, the number of the sacraments has always been a cause of dissension, ever since they began to be numbered in the Middle Ages. The number seven was "canonized" at the Council of Trent in opposition to the reformers' view of baptism and the Lord's Supper as the only sacraments "of divine appointment and perpetual obligation"—though Luther held on for some time to penance as a third. Controversy raged fiercely around this point to the extent that defence of the larger number became practically the touchstone of orthodoxy, as the writing on our coins still testifies. Here at once we can make a useful and extremely simple move towards greater mutual understanding and indeed towards our own understanding of what the sacramental system means, namely, by distinguishing the two great Church sacraments, baptism and the Sacred Meal, from the other five. The difference, of course, is not in degree of efficacy but in their position in the economy of salvation and especially in that they are the great social sacramental acts. Baptism is initiation into the community of the redeemed; the eucharistic assembly, the *synaxis*, is *the* concrete expression of the Church as an ideal entity, the *ecclesia in actu*. This is confirmed by the historical fact that the early Christian communities were identified during the first two or three centuries by their sacred and mysterious meal taken in common, and therefore confused with the *hetaeriae* or cult associations, mostly of Eastern origin, which were then proscribed.[1]

[1] Especially clear in Pliny's letter to the Emperor Trajan. See Newman, *Development of Christian Doc-*

This distinction, vital for our understanding of structure, is seen more clearly with reference to the development in sacramental doctrine which lies behind the presence of the seven sacraments in our Catechism. Confirmation emerges as the fullness of baptism and penance as the answer to grave sin committed after baptism. Orders has meaning only with reference to a special delegation to the Eucharist as a sacrifice. All this took some time to clarify; more so with marriage and the anointing of the sick, neither of which is mentioned directly in the Gospels. One can see that only on condition of our making this distinction and accepting its consequences does our position become, if not acceptable, at least credible, to our fellow Christians with whom we are speaking. It also brings our attention to bear firmly on the one vital point of divergence, namely, the relation between Gospel and Church, especially in the case of Anglicans, since they fully accept, in the formula of the Revised Catechism, "other sacramental ministries of grace provided in the Church" as distinct from "sacraments which Christ, in the Gospel, appointed for his Church". Newman, in a masterly chapter in his *The Development of Christian Doctrine*, demonstrated

---

trine, New Ark Library ed., Sheed and Ward (1960), pp. 152ff.

this very forcibly with particular reference to the sacraments.[1]

A quite different set of difficulties arises, for ourselves as well as for other Christians, in the kind of language, sanctioned by age-long usage, which we employ in describing what a sacrament is and what its function consists in within the context of the Christian life. This is a wide and complicated subject to which we can only allude in the form of two examples. In the first place, the Aristotelian categories of matter and form (hylomorphism), of undoubted utility for the task of theological articulation, have raised some difficulties in their application to the sacraments. Thus theologians can speak only of a *quasi-materia* of penance; the long dispute, in which Anglican scholars have played a part, over what was the form of orders was only solved by an authoritative statement in 1947; and, in the case of matrimony, we have the truly desperate expedient of regarding the mutual and exclusive right to intimacy and the acceptance of that right as, respectively, the matter and form of that sacrament. A second example might be the use of the scholastic formula *ex opere operato* to describe the peculiar efficacy of the sacramental action. This is not only rather inaccessible in itself but has also, consciously or unconsciously, induced a way of think-

[1] Newman, *Development*, pp. 68–9.

ing on this subject which has made it too easy to
think of a sacrament as a kind of supernatural
slot-machine requiring of us, in terms of personal
commitment or participation, nothing more than
working a lever. As Louis Bouyer remarks:

> Even today, despite all the progress made
> since the sixteenth century, can we deny that
> there is only too often, in our sacramental prac-
> tice, superstition in disguise? Many Catholics,
> even the very devout, would seem to think that
> holiness for them was in direct proportion to
> the number of their Communions, even if they
> make no personal effort to receive the sacra-
> ment with fervour. And how many Catholics
> are there who have Masses said to obtain, come
> what may, something they are anxious for,
> even if its moral goodness is at least doubtful,
> and who expect therefrom a quasi-automatic
> result as if from some magical practice?[1]

In addition to difficulties arising out of terminology there is this other, which is felt in all sectors
of our theology, that the history of any particular
treatise, the heresies which have had to be com-
bated, the debates, sometimes lasting for centuries,
to which it has given rise, leave their mark on the
manner in which it is presented to us, sometimes

[1] *The Word, Church and Sacraments in Protestantism
and Catholicism*, Geoffrey Chapman (1961), p. 67.

to the extent of upsetting the original proportions and structure. An example which comes to mind is the large part which is occupied in the treatise concerning grace by the controversies over the reconciliation of divine grace and human will, reflecting the long and at times fierce *de-auxiliis* controversy beginning in the sixteenth century. It is therefore not altogether surprising if ordinary Christian people, in thinking about the sacraments, sometimes tend to miss the wood for the trees. A reading of 1 Corinthians, where the feeling for and conviction of the presence of the risen Christ in the Church as a mystery to be shared in and lived is so strong, would take us back at once to the point from which all the sacraments begin and take their meaning. After all, rites and ceremonies and even the precise specification of matter and form have changed considerably in the long history of the Church; moreover, God is not in any way obliged to communicate himself in what we call the life of grace within the framework of the sacraments—there is also the uncovenanted self-giving, though always through his word. Our Christian life is not to be taken as a set of rules and pious practices which include "going to the sacraments", but God present to us in the life and death of Jesus, from which everything else flows.

In its religious and biblical context the word *sacramentum*, as used in the Vulgate translation of Jerome, translates the Greek word *mysterion*. But this mystery takes its meaning from the whole field of life and experience, not just from intellectual activity, as in the Catechism definition of "a truth which is above reason but revealed by God". In every significant human encounter there is something of this mystery; it can be experienced though not really analysed or understood at the moment when, for example, a real friendship suddenly comes into existence or when love is born. Much more so when a person experiences in some way a relationship with God which is truly an encounter with him as a person, not just as a theorem to be proved. This is describing it subjectively, from our own point of view; but the mystery we are speaking about implies that God comes to us, and in a way adapted to the complexity of our nature and our situation in both the visible and invisible worlds. The Christian believes that this encounter of the eternal God with us is effected in Christ in whom the grace, the gift, takes on visible form—a truth which can be said to be the *Leitmotiv* of the Liturgy, especially in the East, and which finds classical expression in the Preface of the Nativity. Christ is the one mediator between God and us, between the visible and the invisible worlds;[1] the Mystery, therefore, which is our encounter with the living

[1] 1 Tim. 2.5.

and life-giving God, must take place through and in him.

We can follow up how Paul works this out for the benefit of his Corinthian Christians. They are "sanctified in Christ Jesus" (1.2), the grace of God is given them "in Christ Jesus", with him they have "fellowship" (1.9). The encounter, the Mystery, must be effected at this point. Paul says the same thing when he defines Christ as "the power of God" (1.24)—"power" meaning the ability to produce a real effect, a real change within our earthly existence. This power is communicated through the Gospel as the word of God which comes to us from the Church. The question arises, however, as to how in practice the Church makes it possible for us to experience this living encounter with God. Perhaps we can look for an answer to this question by drawing a parallel between the sacraments and the Gospel miracles. When the Baptist sent an embassy to Jesus to ask about his real identity the answer came: "Tell John what you have seen and heard: the blind see, the lame walk, lepers are cured, the deaf hear, the dead are raised and the poor have the good news proclaimed to them."[1] What the answer means is that in Jesus the divine reality which constitutes the last age, the kingdom of God, is already somehow present, since it is really

[1] Matt. 11.4–5.

nothing else but a free version of an Isaian prophecy of the age to come:

> Then the eyes of the blind shall be opened
> And the ears of the deaf unstopped;
> Then shall the lame man leap like the hart,
> And the tongue of the dumb sing for joy.[1]

The miracles were signs of a divine power at work, a mediation into the visible world of the eternal and invisible God; while, in fact, the Synoptics usually make use of the synonym "power" (*dynamis*) for miracle, John's Gospel speaks of "signs" (*semeia*). In the same way, the sacraments are signs of the new and final dispensation into which the Christian has entered through Church membership; they constitute an experience of "the powers of the age to come".[2]

Having established a basis for our understanding of the meaning, structure and development of sacramental life in the Church, we can go on to consider them singly with the particular purpose of getting some idea of their organic relationship one to another and the part they play in the dynamism of the Christian life. Without making any attempt at being exhaustive or systematic, we shall see what this letter tells us about the two great Church sacraments, recognized as such

[1] Isa. 35.5–6.
[2] Heb. 6.5.

from the beginning, and what seeds of future development from these two can be discerned.

1. BAPTISM

The most obvious difference between baptism then and now is the severance of the moments of baptism and conversion in the great majority of cases today. It is the norm in the New-Testament period for baptism to follow and put the seal on conversion, but this is now the rule only in the small majority of adult baptisms. Here, however, a double source of possible misunderstanding must be removed. Though there is no explicit mention in New-Testament texts of a particular child being baptized, there is every reason to believe that, for example, when Paul baptized the household of Stephanas (1.16) the children also were included. On the other hand, infant baptism as practised today, far from being anything of an embarrassment for the theologian or biblical scholar, provides a splendid illustration of two vitally important aspects of life in the Church: the idea of corporate responsibility and the baptismal event as coextensive with the whole life-span of the baptized. In the person of the godparent the whole Church puts its faith at the disposal of the infant unconscious of what is going on—a profound and fecund idea which has permeated the whole of the Roman liturgy, even beyond the prayers which have grown up round this sacrament; as for the second aspect, it is sufficient to note for the time being the frequent use of the aorist tense in reference to baptism, with its implication of an effect which continues operative down to the present.[1] Despite all this, it is obvious that we run the risk, under these changed circumstances, of forgetting much more easily the vital role of baptism in our existence as Christians, not to mention the danger of the sacrament being taken merely as a social custom, unaccompanied by any real faith and therefore void of effect.

Much can be learnt about the real meaning of Christian initiation by simply looking at the long catalogue of synonyms for the term "Christian" which we come across in reading this letter— many of them directly referring to baptism. The Christian is sanctified (1.2), that is, set aside from the world; he is one of the saints (the same basic meaning, 1.2; 6.2); he is summoned out of the world, for baptism is for him the divine call (1.2,9; 7.17–18); he is washed, sanctified, justified (6.11); in baptism he has been bought and then set free, as a wealthy and benevolent nobleman might pay the price for a slave in order to give him his freedom (6.20; 7.23).

This last point is significant in that it represents

[1] Especially of the verb *pisteuo*, believe; e.g., Acts 19.2.

baptism as a great liberating act while at the same time emphasizing the principle of corporate personality basic to a true theology of the Church. In the Old Testament it was a primary duty of a blood relation to free his kinsman from slavery should he have had the misfortune to fall into it —this idea of group responsibility is in fact a basic sociological feature of Hebrew, as it is of Teutonic, society, quite apart from any religious or theological implications. This is the context in which we should understand the term "Redeemer" used of the Covenant-God, and it was in the great saving event of the Exodus that the redemption of Yahweh's people, his kinsmen, took place. This Exodus, the great social experience out of which we can say the whole of the Hebrew Scriptures grew, the story of which is kept alive year by year in the Passover *haggada*, is the type of the saving act of God "with a mighty hand and outstretched arm" in the passion and death of Jesus. It is, therefore, not surprising that baptism, which is "into his death",[1] should be described as an Exodus.

Our fathers were all under the cloud, and all passed through the sea, and all were baptized into Moses in the cloud and in the sea ... nevertheless with most of them God was not pleased. [10.1–5.]

[1] Rom. 6.3.

It does not set man free on the economic or
political or moral level, but strikes at the very
roots of the determinism of his natural existence;
above all, it frees him from the burden of his past.

> Was any of you at the time of his call already
> circumcised? Let him not seek to remove the
> marks of circumcision. Was any one at the time
> of his call uncircumcised? Let him not seek
> circumcision. For neither circumcision counts
> for anything nor uncircumcision, but keeping
> the commandments of God. [7.18–19.]

> Neither circumcision counts for anything nor
> uncircumcision, but a new creation. [Gal. 6.15.]

> If anyone is in Christ he is a new creation.
> [2 Cor. 5.17.]

What you were before does not count; this is a
new country, a new age.

The trinitarian form now obligatory at baptism
and found at the end of the First Gospel and
also in the first-century Church book called the
Didache (only one of numerous similarities) is not
in fact used in the baptisms mentioned in the Acts
and would appear to represent a later stage of
development, some of the history of which can
be filled in. Thus, when speaking of their baptism,
Paul says to the Christians of Corinth, "You
were justified in the name of the Lord Jesus
Christ and in the Spirit of our God" (6.11), the

three Persons are mentioned. The starting-point in the perception of faith is Jesus in his death and resurrection as the living act of the Father; and just as the giving of the Spirit to the Church at Pentecost is dependent on the Resurrection and Ascension, so for each individual Christian the Spirit only comes after he has been identified, after he has found his true identity, in that saving act.[1] During the earliest days baptism was "in the name of Jesus",[2] and it was disagreement over the name (that is, person) with whom one entered into association at baptism, which had caused all the trouble at Corinth. (1.10ff.) This phrase, "Jesus is *Kyrios*", is, moreover, a miniature confession of faith in the Resurrection, in the name he received from the Father as the risen Lord, for Paul the whole centre of faith *as such*, faith even in the existence of God. For Paul, everything hangs by this one thread and he is willing to accept with ruthless logic the consequences:

If Christ has not been raised, then our preaching is in vain and your faith is in vain. We are even found to be misrepresenting God, because we testified of God that he raised Christ, whom he did not raise if it is true that the dead are not raised. For if the dead are not

[1] Rom. 6.3–4.
[2] Acts 2.38; 4.12; 8.16; 10.48; 16.33.

raised then Christ has not been raised. [15.14–16.]

This gives some idea of the part that faith plays in baptism, which is baptism *into* the death of the Lord crowned by his resurrection; and why so often the verb "to believe" is used simply as a synonym for being baptized.

This consecration implied by the constant reference to the "name", and now for us every time that we make the sign of the Cross, is sealed by what theologians have called, since the time of Innocent III, the sacramental character of baptism. Underlying the rather inaccessible imagery of a mark or seal put upon the soul conceived of as a solid substance there is the idea of a permanent association with Christ who, as Priest, recapitulates the function of the whole human race in the praise and worship of God. According to St Thomas, the Christian, in baptism, receives a deputation to share in the sacerdotal function of Christ, an insight taken up by Luther in his doctrine of the priesthood of all the faithful, which, in recent times, now shorn of its polemical undertones, we can accept as a valid insight, rooted in the Scriptures and patristic tradition.[1] Both Baptism and the Eucharist

[1] Basic texts for the "seal of the Spirit" are 2 Cor. 1.22; Eph. 1.13. There is a general reawakening of interest in this subject today outside the Catholic Church

therefore lead back to Christ as head and representative of the redeemed community.

2. CONFIRMATION

The universality of infant baptism has had the effect of leaving confirmation in something of a vacuum, since for Catholics it is conferred ideally at the time of coming to the use of reason, while for Anglicans, for example, it is in practice associated with the Eucharist. This is the result of the vicissitudes of the Church's history. During the time of the catechumenate confirmation was always seen as the fullness of baptism and was conferred immediately after it, as can be seen from a canon of the Council of Elvira at the beginning of the fourth century which stipulated that in the case of emergency baptism of a sick or dying catechumen he should be brought to the bishop upon recovery "so that through the imposition of hands he might be perfected".[1] The time-gap between the two sacraments—which was there from the beginning, as in the account of the conversion of the Samaritans[2]—should not therefore distract us from the very real relation between them.

---

as well as inside; see the *Report of Anglican-Methodist Conversations*, p. 23.

[1] Denzinger, para. 52.

[2] Acts 8.14ff.

This is seen in the conferring of the Holy Spirit in this sacrament, which makes it something of a Pentecost for the individual receiving the sacrament, enabling him to go down into the arena of life in the world and speak and act with boldness and decision as did the first Christians after their experience during the Feast of Weeks. Already with Paul there are signs that in addition to baptism being "in the name of the Lord Jesus" it was also "in the Spirit of our God" (6.11), the presence of which Spirit was so often attested by visible signs, sometimes even before the actual baptismal rite had been administered.[1] As far as confirmation is concerned, this invocation of and consecration to the Spirit has to take on some of the force which it has in the Old-Testament stories of Gideon, Samson and Saul, upon whom the Spirit comes mightily, especially in moments of danger or emergency, a force from beyond them which takes them further than their natural limitations allow; and, from the very nature of the case, crisis is endemic to the life of the Christian in the world.

It would be a pity, though, if we took a purely supernaturalist view of what happens in this or, for that matter, any other sacrament. Moral progress comes about by actualizing all the forces and potentialities of nature, of man foursquare,

[1] As in the case of Cornelius and his household, Acts 10.44ff.

as such. This is implied in all the sacramental rites by what is called the *matter* of each of them. In this case anointing with oil and, more directly, the laying on of hands. The coming of the Spirit is not an end but a beginning, a starting-point for a period of moral struggle in which the adolescent has to learn to face the intractable facts of environment and temperament in order to emerge *approved*, a man of character. Thus, even the internecine strife within the Corinth community is seen as serving a providential purpose: "There must be factions among you in order that those who are genuine among you may be recognized." (11.19.) Later on, writing in the same city to a Church he had not founded, that of Rome, he developed this further:

> We rejoice in our sufferings, knowing that suffering produces endurance, and endurance produces character, and character produces hope, and hope does not disappoint us, because God's love has been poured into our hearts through the Holy Spirit which has been given to us.[1]

But since this kind of endurance, positive endurance of the world, is not possible without Christian perception, in the great complex act in which the Christian dies and is buried with Christ to his past this gift of sight is also implied—"Now we

[1] Rom. 5.3–5.

5

have received not the spirit of the world, but the Spirit which is from God, that we might understand the gifts bestowed on us by God." (2.12.) This is all well summed up in the words of the Anglican Catechism about confirmation giving "strength for the Christian life".

One last point of a practical nature. Since confirmation is the fullness of baptism we could argue, as in fact many are now doing, that the best time for its reception would be when we might most reasonably expect the serious conversion of life to take place, the fuller realization of the meaning of the Christian life and the renunciations it involves. It is questionable whether this coincides with the arrival at the use of reason. Its exact determination is too large a question to discuss here; but a rite carried out with full solemnity and with adequate preparation just before school-leaving would certainly appear to mean more and to fulfil better the ends of the sacrament than is the case under the present ordering.

3. CONFESSION

Baptism frees the Christian at one blow from the chains of the past because it frees him from sin; it is "unto the remission of sins", and was accompanied by a public confession of sin. No-one who has been given his freedom wishes to return to slavery—that is the point of Paul's magnificent statement on baptism to the Romans (6.1–11) where the baptized is said to enter into "newness of life". Within this perspective confession could not become a normal routine element in Christian life. This is plain from the discipline of the early Church in the case of grave sin, in particular in the question of apostasy and the *traditio calicis* or *librorum*; it appears in the view of the convert Essene Hermas that there could be in practice only one more chance after baptism, and it is apparent in some particularly thought-provoking passages in the New Testament itself. In whatever context we choose to understand the warning which we find in the Epistle to the Hebrews there can be no doubting its seriousness:

> It is impossible to restore again to repentance those who have once been enlightened [that is, baptized], who have tasted the heavenly gift, and have become partakers of the Holy Spirit, and have tasted the goodness of the Word of God and the powers of the age to come, if they then commit apostasy, since they crucify the Son of God on their own account and hold him up to contempt. [6.4–6.]

Thus, as with confirmation, we are led to think of what penance means in the Christian's life in the light of baptism; for Luther, writing in his *Babylonish Captivity*, it was "a way back to baptism", a definition which, freed from the polemical context in which it was uttered, we can accept as valid.

But of course people go on sinning after baptism and even in the very earliest days of the Church's history, despite the living witness to Christ which the Apostles gave, despite the hope of an imminent end to the interim period, there had to be a dispensation of pardon. Even the Christian guilty of incest is treated severely so that "his spirit may be saved in the day of the Lord Jesus" (5.5)—it is therefore a medicinal penalty, though there is much obscure in the way it is described. It does not require a very deep reading of this letter to see that there must have been pretty frequent need for contrition and absolution on account of backsliding of one kind or another, and we have a letter of Clement of Rome written to this same Church about a generation later which enjoins on them obedience to the "presbyters" in accepting correction as penance for their sins, in particular those of discord and schism. After all, what Paul asks—and what is still asked today—to keep the heart free for God, to avoid attachments and the anxiety (a crucial Pauline word) which they bring, to possess *as if not* possessing, to be in the world and yet free of it, to "care and not to care"—all this is very hard, and for them as for us there is the frequent backward glance, the *nostalgie de la boue*. It is in this sacrament that Christian realism and humility show at their best.

It might be said that one of the aspects about the practice of confession in the Church in our days which cause uneasiness is the tendency to expect from the frequentation of it a kind of automatic effect, more so, perhaps, than with any other of the sacraments. This is abetted by the pronunciation (often rapid) of a formula in a language unknown to the penitent and the more or less standardized "penance" imposed—three "Hail Marys" or something similar. There is also the fact that many penitents exhaust their spiritual energies in trying to distinguish between grave and venial sin and leave little time or energy for contrition and amendment. Various suggestions for improving the practice of penance have been and are being made: use of the vernacular (now allowed in principle), more realistic and up-to-date penances, revitalization of the eucharistic con-fession of sin (it should surely be brought for-ward immediately before the Offertory) and so on—but a thoughtful comparison of our practice with that of the earliest days, as presumed also though not explicit in this letter, would certainly go some way to bringing about an insight into the meaning of the sacrament in the context of the Christian life, without which insight any reform of the kind contemplated would be a waste of time.

4. EUCHARIST

It is precisely because the Eucharist today seems so different from what it was in the first century that a study of what Paul tells us about it in Corinthians can be so rewarding. It is not just the structure of the service which has been altered; hidden currents of thought, philosophical speculation, theological debate have all taken their toll. It is sufficient to mention the great emphasis placed on the *praesentia physica* of Christ *in* the sacrament in reaction to the theory of Berengar in the eleventh century, or the profound influence on the way people view the sacrament exerted by individualism and subjectivism in modern times. As far as structure is concerned, we might simply recall how the introduction of the Elevation in the medieval period, with the consequent isolation of the words of institution, broke up the unity of the Great Prayer and created, in the minds of many Mass-goers at least, a climax which left the *eating and drinking* high and dry. With the use of bells, gongs and even electronic devices in some countries to underline and emotionally overcharge this isolated moment in the Mass, we can easily imagine how it could come to be considered, by some of the faithful, as little more than a magical act worked on their behalf by the priest.

Is the answer simply to reintroduce the Eucharist as celebrated in Paul's day? Of course not; in fact, even then there were abuses which had to be got rid of. The Eucharist stands in something like the same relation to the Church as does tradition; in fact, we can consider it as a type of tradition, a living voice by which Jesus, through the Word and the Spirit, speaks to us in the Church. The very fact that the Church has introduced words of her own even into the words of institution should put us on our guard against a simplicist solution.[1] It remains true none the less that the Church's thinking on the Eucharist and her pastoral concern shown in movements of reform must be absolutely regulated by the Scriptures, and it is here that the work of understanding and penetration comes in.

We have already, in the chapter on Church unity, discussed the Eucharist as the *sacramentum unitatis, the* Church sacrament, and in the last chapter, on Liturgy and life, still have to see something about it as an action involving the whole assembly. We can therefore confine our attention here to the description of the service given by Paul and to one or two points of interpretation which frequently arise in inter-Church dialogue.

---

[1] In the preliminary section *qui pridie quam pateretur* is not in any Gospel account, while *et elevatis oculis in coelum* is taken from the "eucharistic" miracle of the Feeding of the Five Thousand; Mark 6.41 etc. In the words of institution themselves *mysterium fidei* is added.

The account of the Lord's Supper in 11.23–34 is the first, chronologically, which we possess and therefore obviously of great importance. Paul stresses right at the beginning that the Eucharist is *traditioned*—"I received from the Lord what I also handed on to you . . ."—not as doctrine but as a command to perform an action. In the words of the Lord the imperative is used four times—it is therefore a commandment like one of the Ten Commandments, not just an exhortation to perform a devotional exercise; it must be of the essence of Church life. The command is also addressed to the community—*Do this*—eat and drink—and the proclamation of the Lord's death, through all the interim period until his coming, is performed in and through the act of eating and drinking on the part of the gathered assembly and should therefore speak for itself without need of explanation or interpretation. This is already quite different in emphasis from phrases like "saying Mass", "assisting at Mass" and the like.

It is all the more necessary for us to think deeply on the meaning of this account—the Eucharist as a community action, as a memorial service of the Lord's death, as an anticipation of his glorious coming and the triumph of God's kingdom—on account of the decline in our corporate sense and the lively expectation of the Lord's coming of the kind which animated the Corinthian community. There is also the added difficulty that, with Communion under one kind only, the direct symbolism of death within the action is no longer apparent. The result often is that routine takes over and the Eucharist becomes just another devotional act, like saying the Rosary or going to Benediction. Paul warns against this in the little scriptural homily in which he uses the by then common analogy between the Eucharist and the manna in the desert. He says that all of the People of God ate of the spiritual, God-given food, and yet "with most of them God was not pleased" (10.5)—a clear warning against attributing automatic efficacy to frequent and even daily frequentation of the Eucharist in the absence of the right dispositions. There is, therefore, no ontological level of operation of grace in our lives distinct and apart from our own intentions and personal involvement; not to admit this is to have already crossed over the boundary between religion and superstition. It is apparent also, in the case of Christians at Corinth, that many had neglected this; they had taken part in the service carelessly, out of habit, even in a disorderly fashion, and had not "discerned the Body" (11.29)—with the sad results which Paul goes on to mention.

The question of discerning the Body leads us on to a different point, one so complex that it can only be touched on or outlined here. The interpretation of this and the other eucharistic texts in the New Testament has been at the storm centre of inter-Church relations for the last 400 years. Two questions have always been of decisive importance: Whether the Eucharist is a sacrificial action or merely a memorial service; *how* Christ is present in the sacrament. We can do no more here than point to one or two things that Paul says to his Christians at Corinth on the subject of the eucharistic assembly and try to ask the right kind of question arising from this.

On the first point, we must state clearly that in this letter the element of memorial service is dominant. This is seen in particular in the command to do the action as a memorial (11.24)[1] and the clear statement that the act of eating and drinking must *proclaim* the Lord's death (11.26). But if, through the memorial service, this death is somehow present as a mystery to be shared in, will it not be present in its essential nature, as sacrifice? Will not the meal be a sacrificial meal? It is certain that sacrificial terminology is used of the Eucharist in the early Church—the word *thusia* ("sacrifice"), the use of the well-known prophecy of Malachy about a clean oblation.[2] In warning them away from pagan rites (10.14–21)

---

[1] The *anamnesis* seems to translate the Jewish liturgical term *zikkaron*, which means precisely a memorial service.

[2] Mal. 1.11–12. This quite apart from the question of the literal sense of the prophecy.

he compares the eating and drinking in the Eucharist with the Jewish sacrificial meal and heathen sacrifices to the gods. In other words, he places the Eucharist in the same pattern of union with the deity through sharing in a cultic meal. It is interesting that in this passage *both* the controversial words "altar" and "table" occur side by side. Also, in another passage, he compares himself to the ministers of the Old Dispensation who served at the altar. (9.13.) All this, of course, would tell us very little in itself about what the sacrificial act really means and entails—for which we should have to range over the whole of the New-Testament literature. But it would seem to justify our going beyond a merely metaphorical sense such as is found in the Anglican Catechism definition, which speaks of a "sacrifice of praise".

The question of the presence of Christ in the Eucharist, what Catholics refer to as the Real Presence, really concerns *how* he is present, since no Christian would deny presence of some kind. For some, the presence will be no more than that which he promised when two or three gather together in his name; others think of a spiritual presence at the meal, rather like the Messiah at the Jewish Passover meal or the sectarian meal of the Qumran community; others again speak of Christ's mysterious presence, at the saving moment of his death, but only within the action which re-presents, that is, makes present again, that saving moment. To discuss this question satisfactorily we should have to go through all the eucharistic texts in the New Testament and early Christian literature. Within the limits imposed by our discussion we can only ask whether Paul, in contrasting the reality of the relationship entered into at the eucharistic celebration with the nothingness of pagan gods and what is offered to them (10.16–19), does not go beyond all this; we should also point to the solemn warning about being guilty "of the body and blood of the Lord" and the failure to "discern the Body" (11.27–9). Even if some explanations of theologians, especially in the Middle Ages, have not been very helpful or if popular piety has at times exaggerated, these words must be given their full weight.

5. HOLY ORDER

This letter does not tell us much, at first reading, about the sacrament of order as we understand and are familiar with it in the Church today. The name is, of course, never used; Corinth is never called a diocese, there is no mention of a bishop or of assistant priests and no sign of a clergy-laity division. Even when he is talking of the weekly liturgical gathering, Paul never gives us the name of the president or priest or even suggests directly that there was one present.

There are, of course, reasons for this. The full explicitation of this sacrament, as of the other four which are in one way or another in function of baptism or the Eucharist, does not take place at once. If we read the letter of Clement to the same Church about a generation later we shall find plenty of evidence of organization and of Church leaders who exercise the power of orders. From the time of the Pastoral Epistles there is no lack of evidence of the ordination of bishops with their assistants in the local Churches; Timothy, to whom two of the letters are addressed, is an example. As long as the expectation of the imminent return of the risen Lord was right in the forefront of people's minds there was little room for long-term planning, organization and providing for the power given to the Apostles to be handed on to successors.

At the same time we might, in view of some unhappy chapters in the history of clergy-laity relationships, permit ourselves a little nostalgia on looking back at that small, fervent, *possessed* Christian community. It gives us an example of what we should never have lost as the result of clerical preponderance in certain periods of the Church's history—in particular, the wide distribution of functions, especially charismatic functions, in Church life and the strong sense of corporate existence and activity based on a common baptized status. At any rate, the emphasis at Corinth was certainly on liberty even at the expense of order. We can only speculate whether the leader of the community was Stephanas (1.16; 16.15) or someone else, or whether the leaders of the parties mentioned at the beginning of the letter were ordained. There is also the question of whom Paul is referring to when he speaks of "the cup of blessing which we bless" and "the bread which we break" (10.16–17)—whether he is speaking in the sense of "we priests" or of the community in general as represented by the president, since evidently not all break the bread.

It is true that at various times since the Reformation (and possibly before) people have pointed to early Christian Churches like that of Corinth as blessedly priestless societies and have made much of the fact that the word *hiereus*, priest, is never used of a Christian minister in the New Testament. The answer to this has usually been that the word was avoided in order not to confuse the Christian with the Old-Testament ministry; but perhaps this does not go deep enough. It is plain that the old liturgical order was completely superseded in the new and final worship of God in Christ—suffice it to recall the Lord's saying on the Temple.[1] With this went also the priestly caste which had been at the

[1] John 2.19–21.

service of the old order and against which there had risen up a violent reaction of popular and religious piety at the time of our Lord, a reaction many traces of which can be found also in the New Testament.[1] We should have to read the Epistle to the Hebrews in order to see how the heavenly Christ is the one high priest of the new order and how, in his worship of the Father, which is the vehicle of the worship of the Christian Church, is radicalized whatever was of value in the old order. This is the one and only Christian worship and all Christians share in it if in different ways. The sacramental seal or character of baptism, by which one becomes a member of the priestly people,[2] confers a permanent right and duty to take part in this worship; the character of orders confers, over and above this, a special delegation to share in this eternal priesthood of the risen Lord, but in function of the baptized community. It does not confer admittance to a priestly caste over against or simply over the Christian community—something which has at times been forgotten with great loss to the Church and the spiritual life of its members.

[1] The evidence for this is well known to scholars and has to be sought in the inter-testamentary literature including that of Qumran. Perhaps the most striking case in the New Testament is the speech of Stephen, Acts 7.
[2] 1 Pet. 2.5,9; Exodus 19.6. See also Chapter 7.

6. ANOINTING OF THE SICK

There is good evidence in the early-Church period for pastoral care of the sick and the practice of healing. In both "lists" of charismatic gifts exercised in the Corinthian community healing is mentioned.[1] In the account of the apostolic mission in Mark[2] we are told that many sick were anointed with oil and so cured, and the practice is explicitly enjoined in the catholic epistle of James.[3] Here the sick man (there is no mention of danger of death) is advised to call Church leaders to his bedside who will pray over him and anoint him with oil in the name of the Lord. This action, if performed with faith, will bring about his cure and the remission of any sins of which he may have been guilty.

It is in this text of James that Catholic theology has seen most clearly the sacramental possibilities of such an action. There is the outward, symbolic act of anointing with oil, *the* healing medicament in antiquity,[4] with the word of power, the invocation of the name of the Lord, and the faith without which any sacramental action becomes a mere charade. It is well known how Luther rejected this letter and therefore the sacrament of anoint-

[1] 12.9 and 28.
[2] Mark 6.13.
[3] Jas. 5.14–15.
[4] See in the story of the Prodigal Son, Luke 10.34; cf. Isa. 1.6.

ing with it, and how Protestant theology has refused to consider such healing as sacramental because not in the Gospel. Difficulties have been increased by the use, since the twelfth century, of the term "extreme unction": the substantive means something different in modern English and the adjective is really inappropriate since the sacrament has been primarily connected with the imminent danger of death only by historical accident. It is interesting and encouraging to note a great revival of interest in this sacrament among both Catholics and Anglicans—the latter, however, refer to it, as to confirmation, as a "ministry".

One thing we should note is how, for these early Christians, the whole of their existence, including sickness and death, is drawn into the structure of the new life. Thus at Corinth, and doubtless elsewhere, the gift of healing comes from the Spirit which is received at baptism. It carried with it, as we see in James, the forgiveness of sins, which meant a return to baptism. We know from a remark which Paul lets drop in giving them a piece of his mind over the way the eucharistic service was conducted that, as a result of irreverence and perhaps sacrilege, many of them were sick and infirm and some had died. (11.30.) This evidently does not mean, as some have supposed, that in view of the Lord's imminent coming no-one normally would have died. It may be that Paul is referring to a recent epidemic or disaster of some kind which he sees as a divine punishment for their misconduct; but it would be even more consistent to refer it to the gifts of healing which had failed with some of them, which failure demonstrated, for Paul, how the steady flow of the life of the Spirit throughout the community was being blocked. Once again, we are invited to see the sacraments, not as isolated acts, but as functions, articulations, of the one new life in the redeemed community.

7. MARRIAGE

It will be no harm to repeat—and we shall return to this in Chapter 6—that Paul had no intention of composing a treatise on Christian marriage in the manner of a papal encyclical when he wrote to his Christians at Corinth. But he does let drop a hint here and there as to what marriage ought to mean for those who have entered into the Christian newness of life. One case which was bound to come up was of a marriage between non-Christians one of whom comes to accept baptism. What is to happen? The more compelling union is with Christ through baptism, and so if the non-Christian partner seriously menaces this union the marriage is no longer binding. (7.15–17.)[1] But if the partners can continue to

[1] This is known as the Pauline Privilege. It applies only when one partner is converted after a marriage between

live together in concord the marriage continues in force, for the non-Christian partner "is made holy" (7.14) through contact with the other—that is to say, he or she is drawn into the sacred sphere set up by the baptism and Church membership of the other, into the sacramental influence of the body of Christ. The children, too, are within this sphere, that is "holy" (7.14), sharing in the ontological sacrality of the Christian life. Writing a little later on to the same Church he almost blurts out: "I desire your good in the same way that God does", and to prove this apparently violent and intemperate statement he goes on, "for I have given you in marriage to one man, presenting you as a chaste virgin to Christ". (2 Cor. 11.2.) If there is at first sight something of the irrational in this statement (and indeed Paul asks them to put up with his folly before making it) it is the irrationality of the great and stormy prophets of the Old Dispensation who were not afraid to represent the divine love in terms of carnal desire. What Paul has in mind is God as the proud father presenting his unblemished daughter the Church to Christ. This is the inclusive mystery of the Church's union with Christ within which we have to contemplate the marriage of Christians, so that, as we have seen for the

---

non-Christians and the other will not live, in the words of Canon 1120, *pacifice sine contumelia Creatoris.*

other sacraments, matrimony is not just an isolated sacramental act but something which is an articulation of the whole life of the Church. This is laid down explicitly in the Letter to Ephesus, which was where Paul was when he wrote to Corinth—if this is an example of the association of ideas, as it may have been, we can only be deeply thankful for it. The passage deserves quoting in full:

Wives, be subject to your husbands, as to the Lord. For the husband is the head of the wife as Christ is the head of the Church, his body, and is himself its saviour. As the Church is subject to Christ, so let wives also be subject in everything to their husbands. Husbands, love your wives as Christ loved the Church and gave himself up for her, that he might sanctify her, having cleansed her by the washing of water with the word, that he might present the Church to himself in splendour, without spot or wrinkle or any such thing, that she might be holy and without blemish. Even so husbands should love their wives as their own bodies. He who loves his wife loves himself. For no man ever hates his own flesh, but nourishes and cherishes it, as Christ does the Church, because we are members of his body . . . "For this reason a man shall leave his father and mother and be joined to his wife, and the two shall become one." This is a great mystery, and I take it to mean Christ and the Church. [5.22–32.]

The mystery, namely, the sacrament of two in one flesh, derives from its hidden cohesion with the greater mystery of the intimate union of the Church with Christ. This truth should not only show the extraordinary richness and fulfilment at every level in Christian matrimony, but should also dispel any misgivings about Paul's own attitude to which a hasty reading of Corinthians might have given rise.

Other points arising as moral *casus* in our letter can now be dealt with rapidly. There may have been some who were over-keen to break off a marriage contracted before baptism, merely on the grounds of their own convenience. To these Paul repeats, *as a command of the Lord*, the indissolubility of matrimony. (7.10–11.) In view of the long discussion on the Gospel sayings on divorce (within a purely Jewish milieu) and the notorious exceptive clause,[1] it is well to remember this reference of Paul to the Lord's command before any of the extant Gospels came into existence, and that he insists on it even under pressure. The Jewish divorce law was essentially a man's law; among pagans either could divorce without much difficulty; as for slaves, their marriage was not recognized in any case. In the face of this

[1] Matt. 5.32; 19.9.

Paul insists on the Christian marriage relationship as exclusive and permanent precisely because of the mystery which it contains.

It is only when we have really come to grips with Paul's theology of the married state that we ought to read what he says about celibacy, which he considers in the light of the *eschata*, the consummation of the world in the Kingdom of God. Where he seems, here and there, to talk of a wife as something of a nuisance, getting in the way of one's real spiritual life (7.32 for example), we ought to couple it with the Gospel parable about the man who gave as an excuse for not accepting the invitation to the feast that he had married a wife.[1] The feast (as a reading of the whole scene will show at once) is the eschatological banquet, the messianic meal at which the Messiah at last appears. Celibacy is therefore seen as a means of giving the undivided attention to preparing for the Lord's coming—even in our greatly changed perspectives. It will be unnecessary to point out, however, having said this, how full of possible equivocation this situation is; this can be seen, to give just one example, in the fervent devotion to John the Virgin Disciple on the part of certain heretic gnostic groups in the Middle Ages. When Paul wishes that they were all as he is (7.7) we may best understand this as an ardent but implicit

[1] Luke 14.20.

desire for the coming of the Lord when the lesser union and mystery will be consumed and fulfilled in the greater.

Knowledge puffs up, but love builds up
If anyone imagines that he knows something, he
* does not know as he ought to know*
But if one loves God
One is known by him . . .
Let all that you do be done in love.

I want you to be free from anxieties.

Brethren, do not be children in your thinking
Be babes in evil
But in thinking be mature.

Whether you eat or drink
Or whatever you do
Do all to the glory of God.

MORALITY AND MATURITY

I F REFERENCES to this letter figure frequently in
textbooks of moral theology, probably to a
greater extent than any other in the Pauline
corpus, it will be on account of its being made up
to a great extent of answers to different *casus con-
scientiae*. It would be easy, but quite wrong, however, to go on from there to describe Paul's
teaching as casuistic, especially in view of the
pejorative associations which have in the course
of time clustered round this adjective. The casuist
approach to morality attempts to foresee every
possible eventuality and provide a capsuled solution in advance. The norm thus tends to be,
What does the book say? and the weight is thrown
on approved authors as the ultimate criterion.
A purely or predominantly casuist morality is
also static; it tends to think only in terms of an
equilibrium instabile as man's ideal, much in the
manner of the Stoics, and leaves little room for
dynamic factors and for development. At its
worst, it can quite easily leave the moral sense
untouched.

The starting-point for Paul, here as elsewhere,

is the redeemed status of the Christian, not just ethical philosophy in general. This will not be surprising for anyone who has grasped, in reading his correspondence, his readiness to pin everything, even his ultimate faith in God, on the one moment of the Resurrection. Everything hangs by this one thread:

> If Christ has not been raised, then our preaching is in vain and your faith is vain. We are even found to be misrepresenting God because we testified of him that he raised Christ, whom he did not raise if it is true that the dead are not raised. [15.14–15.]

He goes on:

> But *now* Christ has been raised from the dead, the firstfruits of those who sleep. [15.20.]

That small adverb *now*, thematic in contexts of this kind, gives us a swift insight into Paul's whole spiritual orientation. We can call it the Christological or baptismal "now", and it implies that from this point onwards it can no longer be a question of a system, a rule of thumb, which has to be automatically applied, but a mystery to be lived. Those who applied such a system in the spirit of the Pharisees were always in the proximate danger of doing so as a means of achieving that feeling of security within the boundaries of the self which was for Paul the very antithesis of living from the gracious and gratuitous gift of God. That is, in fact, the permanent danger precisely because it so easily becomes the permanent motivation for the juridically minded. The characteristic of the new life in Christ is freedom, since the very nature of the redemptive act is to set free:

> But *now* we are loosed from the law of death wherein we were detained; so that we can serve in newness of spirit and not in the oldness of the letter.[1]

There are, as experience shows, many ways of falling back into "the oldness of the letter", not all of which have been avoided in the course of the Church's history. The Christian law of the Spirit has not the object of circumscribing liberty but of giving it its final expression, a fact which Paul emphasizes time and time again. No-one would deny this in theory of course, but it is what happens in practice which counts.

What we notice in this letter, here as in other respects, is the overwhelming awareness of Christ as present; a sense of exhilaration and newness after the heavy burden of guilt brought on by the overall failure to square up to the demands of the natural and positive law. It is in the light of this that we can understand what Paul really means when he uses expressions such as "the

[1] Rom. 7.6.

law of the spirit of liberty" and speaks of "being in the spirit"; it is summed up very well when he says, writing later on to the same community:

> The Lord is the Spirit; and where the Spirit of the Lord is, there is liberty.[1]

Later still, in his letter to the Roman Church, he will set out in compendious form how the Christian is set free, once he enters the community of the saved through mystical identification with Christ in the moment of his redeeming death, from the force and claims of the Law, from the circumambient forces of sin and the death that sin brings, from the anger of God and from fear. The whole of the Christian life flows from the Christ-event, and we should note that these Corinthian Christians of the first hour did not just think themselves close to this event chronologically; they felt themselves *within* an event which was not yet completed. Like the Apostles on the Mount of Olives, their eyes were directed upwards and the words about the return of the Lord were still loud in their ears.[2] Coming back to the moral question, we must ask ourselves whether we are really in the same situation with reference to this event, with all the immediacy and forceful influence on conduct and moral life which it had for Paul's readers.

[1] 2 Cor. 3.17.
[2] Acts 1.10–11.

We can approach it directly, if a little crudely, this way. Suppose it were to become generally known for certain that the earth was to be destroyed and life as we know it brought to an end suddenly and violently on a certain day in the imminent future—something in the way supposed in the film *The Day the Earth Caught Fire*—we could imagine how this knowledge might well have an immediate and ascertainable bearing upon conduct and moral outlook. Reading this letter and others from the earlier period of Paul's career—those to the Church at Salonika in particular—one has the impression that life in these early communities was lived under the sign of the slogan with which this letter ends— *Maranatha!*, "O Lord, come!"—not of course the chill expectation of the kind alluded to above, but an ardent longing for the coming in glory of the risen Lord. The bearing which this expectation—amounting in many minds to certainty— had upon moral questions is evident. The kind of tensions which it produced can be studied in the questions asked about marriage—"What's the point of getting married if the Lord may be coming tomorrow?" Now it is equally evident that we cannot extrapolate directly from this situation to our own, where the tensions and the perspectives are different, and that we have to use care and prudence in interpreting for ourselves texts such as those where Paul advises everyone to stay put; in particular, where he counsels those who are unmarried to stay unmarried. (7.24–9.) We saw earlier on how Paul's own perspectives on the Second Coming changed considerably as time went on, and we, in our turn, cannot be indifferent to the last two thousand years and the changed understanding of time which they have brought.

Does this mean that we can write off all that Paul says as irrelevant in our changed conditions and with our radically different temporal and spatial ideas? By no means. The coming of the Lord is still the great final reality for us, even if we see it in a different depth of focus and feel the need of interpreting the spatial-temporal metaphors in which Paul and the New Testament as a whole speak of it.[1] And since it remains the goal of our hopes for ourselves personally, for the Church and the whole world order, it must still reflect back a bright beam of light upon the moral character of our lives. In this regard, it might be taken as a promising sign that Christianity in our day is being seen increasingly as a religion of crisis. Whatever criticisms might be levelled from other angles against theologians of existentialist

[1] These require careful analysis and evaluation, e.g., Matt. 24 and the problem of reference to the Fall of Jerusalem; 2 Pet. 3, where it is plain that the end is conceived as a reduction to the cosmic *materia prima* out of which it was then considered that the world was composed.

inspiration, they have certainly had the merit of bringing back to our attention the fact that Christianity is essentially this, a faith for a crisis, and of redefining in the light of this what ought to be the Christian's attitude to, his angle on, the world. This is something which is not only common to the ethical ideas of Bonhoeffer and Bultmann, and which has found popular expression in Tillich's well-known essay "The Shaking of the Foundations", but has made its presence felt also among Catholic thinkers and theologians.

Yet as we read on in this letter with our mind on our own situation in the present century, we might be forgiven for feeling a profound disquiet. Have we Catholics not perhaps succumbed to the temptation of thinking in purely static and chronological terms of the "Last Things"? Are not they for us just *there*, at the end of the road, towards which we are to "keep marching on" in a purely chronological progress? Here, perhaps, a brief exercise in philology might help. The language in which Paul wrote has two words for our word "end" and its associated vocabulary. *Eschaton* means the last in a series and therefore chronologically *the end*. The *eschata* are therefore the "Four Last Things", familiar from devotional literature and parish missions. Good conduct is generally inculcated on the Catholic from his tenderest years with reference to the categories of reward and punishment, hell and heaven. This is good, solid doctrine but the circumstances for its favourable reception are not by any means always present. Quite apart from the danger of distorting the child's idea of God and sowing the seeds of future neuroses, unbalanced and exclusive reference to the "Four Last Things" can have other unfavourable results: it can unconsciously paralyze one's apprehension of the here-and-now, causing us to attach little importance to temporal realities and the significance and destiny of the world; and, more important still, it can conceal the need for development. It is so easy to go on from a consideration of the *eschata* to conclude to the necessity for staying, so to speak, in a state of equilibrium, hoping to keep it up until the end. Whatever else one might say of this attitude, it was certainly not shared by Paul.

The other word for "end" is *telos*—this also refers to the last of a series but in the sense of an event which completes, recapitulates and transcends the series. We might translate "goal" or "consummation". This is the rich theological meaning of the Johannine "last word" on the Cross—*tetelestai,* "It is consummated"—the whole work of redemption was at that moment reaching its climax. Applying this to the Christian, it means that the whole of his life is a progress towards fulfilment, to death and resurrection in the way in which they had already entered experience in the death and resurrection of Jesus. Here again, we are drawn away from a merely preceptive morality, and invited to live in full liberty the Christian mystery to which we are called. Writing to the Christians of Philippi, Paul speaks of trying to "*attain* to the resurrection of the dead", and in so doing reveals the inner dynamics of the Christian life:

> For his sake I have suffered the loss of all things, and count them as refuse, in order that I may gain Christ and be found in him, not having a righteousness of my own, based on law, but that which is through faith in Christ, the righteousness from God which depends on faith; that I may know him and the power of his resurrection, and may share his sufferings, becoming like him in his death, that, if possible, I may attain the resurrection from the dead.[1]

It is in the same teleological sense that Paul speaks in our letter of the setting up of the Kingdom of God as "the end"—the last stage and goal of all redemptive history. There is the resurrection of Christ as prototype; then of those who belong to him; then the Kingdom is delivered over to the Father and this is the *telos*. (15.20–24.) On the other hand, Death is the last (*eschatos*) of a series of enemies which have to be overcome in

[1] Phil. 3.8–11.
6

the process. This is a total and dynamic view of existence which does really influence the living of one's daily life—if one believes in it:

> Why am I in peril every hour? I protest, brethren, by my pride in you which I have in Christ Jesus our Lord, I die every day! What do I gain if, humanly speaking, I fought with beasts at Ephesus? If the dead are not raised, "Let us eat and drink, for tomorrow we die!" [15.30–32.]

Thus life is not just living up to a rule, a standard, a code; it is a continual actualization of the great possibilities opened up by the redemptive event. The Christian ideal is to reach the *telos*, to be, that is, *teleios*—mature, perfect. Here it is evidently not a question of psychological maturity and personal integration—we shall have to turn to this at a later stage—but growing up into the Faith, into Christ, into the mystery of his all-encompassing redemptive presence, and, in doing so, dying through this experience to the lost world of the Self. This possibility is what Paul refers to as the *sophia*, the wisdom of God. (1.24ff.) The end result is that a man, from being carnal, in and *of* this world, becomes spiritual, *pneumatikos*—by a gradual transformation which lasts the whole of life:

> Now the Lord is the Spirit, and where the Spirit of the Lord is, there is freedom. And we

all, with unveiled face, beholding the glory of the Lord, are being changed into his likeness from one degree of glory to another; for this comes from the Lord who is the Spirit.[1]

Morality can have meaning for the Christian only by remaining within this full ontological context of Christian existence.

It would be interesting, if space allowed, to discuss in the light of this the kinds of naturalist and humanist ethic which coexist with the Christian faith in the contemporary world. Whether or not one can have anything more than a purely utilitarian ethic outside of a religious tradition and its eschatological or teleological implications might be discussed. It is certainly true that for the run of men who accept at least implicitly the thesis that "when you're dead you're done", the springs of anything more than a purely utilitarian morality in practice soon dry up. The choice has been fairly constant through recorded history as between the good life, the good time and an anaesthetized existence. What might conceivably cause surprise and dismay to Paul were he present among us today would be the attempt to create a new morality, ostensibly Christian since promulgated by Church leaders, but accommodated pacifically to a society which is no longer

[1] 2 Cor. 3.17–18.

living from the centre of New-Testament revelation.

How does this living within the redemptive event bear upon the Christian's moral life? Does it mean that he has to renounce the world and regard it as evil? Here again Paul gives us a vital lead. Christians have to live in the world (5.10); they are not called upon to renounce the richness and promise which the world, the whole of created reality, including the sensual and the perceptible, offer. What they must not do is to make themselves at home in it, become attached— a truth expressed very well in the Oxyrhynchus saying about the world being a bridge which we must pass over but upon which we must build no house. The fundamental fault is self-assurance and the fundamental virtue detachment. This is the force of Paul's "as-if-not" antitheses in this letter:

> Let those who have wives live as if they had none, and those who mourn as if they were not mourning, and those who rejoice as if they were not rejoicing, and those who buy as if they had no goods, and those who deal with the world as though they had no dealings with it. [7.29–31.]

Making oneself at home in the world as if it were for ever, being surrounded with luxuries which have become necessities, one is drawn inexorably into a determined pattern in which freedom becomes impossible, one is locked into the present and no longer free to look to that future where God waits. The central characteristic of this situation in the world is *anxiety*, what the Gospel of Matthew calls "the anxiety of the present age",[1] different from the kind of anxiety Paul tells us he felt "for all the Churches",[2] rooted in the finite and enclosed temporal existence of man. That the Christian should be free from this anxiety flows from the teaching of the whole of the New Testament. It finds expression in the parable of the Sower, where the seed, the life-giving word, is choked when it falls among the thorns which are the anxieties of the world.[3] Elsewhere, in a context which deals with the *parousia* as imminent, we are warned not to get weighed down with the anxieties of this life.[4] In the Sermon on the Mount we are told expressly not to be "anxious for the morrow".[5] It is therefore understandable that Paul, writing to the Christians of Philippi about the expectation of the return of the Lord, should tell them: "Have no anxiety about anything."[6] It is only when the Christian can look to a future full of hope, in the firm belief that the Lord has risen,

[1] Matt. 13.22.
[2] 2 Cor. 11.28.
[3] Matt. 13.22; Luke 8.14.
[4] Luke 21.34.
[5] Matt. 6.34.
[6] Phil. 4.6.

stands over the course of history and will indeed come again in glory, that this anxiety which is built into finite, contingent existence can be exorcized.

Also here in this letter he insists: "I wish you to be free from anxieties." (7.32.) This does not mean a selfish and fatuous complacency, but rather learning through the gradual assimilation of experience "to care and not to care", to take up an attitude to the world which includes at the same time commitment and detachment.

The words "morality" and "maturity" have been linked together in this chapter-heading in the persuasion that the former cannot be conceived rightly without the latter. The Christian *must* grow; he must progress from the negative of fear, inhibition and servility to the positive of love, expansion and liberty. The whole rub in Christianity is that one must go the whole way, enter into it wholeheartedly, or commit oneself to increasing frustration and tensions. It is a call to enter into the full inheritance of a free and adult person. Here again we meet the same problem of how to understand morality, since this idea of moral and spiritual maturity undergoes a profound and highly interesting development in the New-Testament writings. In those contexts which reflect most immediately the Jewish background —the First Gospel and the Letter of James, for example—a fairly well-defined idea of spiritual perfection emerges, taking the form of the integral fulfilment of the *Torah*, the Jewish law. The words addressed to the young man who desired discipleship—"If you will be *perfect*..." remain of set purpose within the limits of the contemporary Jewish idea of perfection or maturity and embody, of course, something of permanent moral value. The perfect man is he who observes the *Torah* integrally, only this specific idea is expressed in the written Greek gospel by the word *teleios*, which has a wider range of meaning. When in fact Paul uses this word we find envisaged a different type of perfection or maturity which leaves behind the predominant obligational and juridical sense and moves into a new sphere. We who are accustomed to a casuistic outlook to such a considerable extent, might find this a little difficult to evaluate correctly, yet maturity in Paul's sense of the word is impossible for us so long as we are occupied with a minimalist morality—trying to determine how far one can go, what one may or may not do, where the exact boundaries of mortal sin lie. A good example of Paul's approach in practice can be seen in the question of legal claims of one member of the community against another. His solution sweeps past the minimalist and juridical aspects and goes straight to the point:

When one of you has a grievance against a brother, does he dare to go to law before the

> unrighteous instead of the saints?... If you
> have such cases, why do you lay them before
> those who are least esteemed by the Church?
> I say this to your shame. Can it be that there
> is no man among you wise enough to decide
> between members of the brotherhood, but
> brother goes to law against brother, and that
> before unbelievers? [6.1–6.]

It goes to the point by the very terms in which
it is phrased—they are brothers, part of a great
brotherhood, they are *the saints*—a minimalist
solution is therefore excluded right away. Everywhere here one breathes the air of a new, all-
pervading order which has taken the place of
"the letter", the old order based on obligation
and fear. Parallel to this, we find a new type of
perfection or maturity which is presupposed in
one way or another on every page of this letter.

The first thing to be said about this new ideal is
that it is conceived of socially. There is no point
in taking up here the discussion on possible points
of contact with the Mysteries where the *teleios*,
the initiate, the mature one, by the very act of
initiation, entered into a society in which the
members were all equal on the basis of a new and
exclusive status, that of the *mystes*. For one thing,
this idea of the person being able to mature only
as integrated into society is evident throughout
the whole range of Greek thought both in the

classical and Hellenistic periods. It lies behind the
actualization in Paul's day of Aesop's fable of the
body and its parts, the idea of interdependence
within an organic unity, which seems to be the
starting-point of one of Paul's master-images of
the Church; it is presupposed in the Stoic doctrine
of the correspondence between the *anima mundi*
and the *anima humana*, and it had been the basic
postulate of life in the *polis*, as can be seen from
Aristotle's statement that a man who opts out of
society must be either a god or a beast. Some of
these undertones can certainly be heard in Paul,
but what is decisive is the new experience:

His gifts [he says elsewhere] were that some
should be apostles, some evangelists, some
pastors and teachers, for the equipment of the
saints, for the work of the ministry, for building
up the body of Christ, until we all attain to the
unity of the faith and of the knowledge of
the Son of God, *to mature manhood,* to the
measure of the full stature of Christ; *so that we
may no longer be children,* tossed to and fro
and carried about with every wind of doctrine
... rather, speaking the truth in love, *we are
to grow up* in every way into him who is the
head, into Christ, from whom the whole body,
joined and knit together by every joint with
which it is supplied when each part is working

properly, *makes bodily growth* and upbuilds itself in love.[1]

Each one can reach his maturity only in performing his own function in the community and contributing to the whole, to the perfect corporate man, the *Christus totus* of Augustine, which the Church has to produce out of the raw material which unredeemed humanity offers. This gives us good theological motivation for emphasizing the importance of personal relationships in the complex social superstructure and impersonal economic machine of organized life today.[2]

It can easily be seen how this social consciousness provides a dynamism, an impulse to action lacking in the purely individualist and subjective idea of perfection; and if, as is often alleged, both individualism and subjectivity have been too characteristic of Catholic life in recent times, a reading of Paul's letters should take us some way to a more balanced outlook.

---

[1] Eph. 4.11–16.

[2] Well brought out in the recent Penguin publication of M. V. C. Jeffreys, *Personal Values in the Modern World*, Harmondsworth, Penguin Books (1962). He sees Christianity's relevance in our modern world along the line of personal relationships: "We cannot of our own power love one another as we ought. But the grace of God comes into human life through the relations between persons; these are the growing-points of the spiritual life." (p. 166.)

To turn to another, related point. The whole question of maturity in Christian living has often been confused by reference to the way of spiritual childhood and the Lord's saying about little children. It is all a question of the context within which this is understood, and while it would not do to get involved in an old-fashioned bout of textual pugilistics, we have Paul's warning to the Christians at Corinth:

> Brethren, do not be children in your thinking; be babes in evil, but in thinking be mature. [14.20.]

Religion in general is the area of maximum reality but also of maximum illusion, and it is a fact of ordinary observation and experience that much that passes for religious behaviour and attitude proceeds in reality from retarded psychological development, unconsciously nourished neuroses and the unresolved conflicts and tensions of early life.[1] In short, the childlike and the infantile have to be carefully distinguished in practice, and this is not always done.

---

[1] This is fortunately being increasingly taken account of by spiritual writers, e.g., Robert W. Gleason, S.J., *To Live is Christ* (1962): "To function maturely requires progressive liberation from the subrational aggressive and sexual impulses of the child-world" (p. 51); "Maturation is a constantly developing process involving the dissolution of infantile complexes." (p. 64.)

The Christian must therefore also grow up intellectually in his faith. When Paul tells his people to be mature in thinking (14.20), this advice goes beyond the immediate context, which deals with the use and abuse of the ecstatic gifts, and implies that they should accept fully the responsibilities of intelligence. It was, after all, precisely because they had failed to grasp with their minds the implications of their baptism that unity had been threatened at Corinth in the first place:

But I, brethren, could not address you as spiritual men but as men of the flesh, as babes in Christ. I fed you with milk not solid food; for you were not ready for it; and even yet you are not ready, for you are still of the flesh. [3.1–2.]

We have the same kind of language used in the Letter to the Hebrews:

About this [that is, the priesthood of Christ] we have much to say which is hard to explain, since you have become dull of hearing. For though by this time you ought to be teachers, you need someone to teach you again the first principle of God's word. You need milk, not solid food; for every one who lives on milk is unskilled in the word of righteousness, for he is a child. But solid food is for the mature, for

those who have their faculties trained by practice to distinguish good from evil.[1]

It is evidently not just a question of understanding
alone, a mere exercise of the intellect, otherwise
we fall into the Socratic heresy; it concerns the
ability to evaluate and distinguish, the development of the intuitive sense of truth. It is, as
experience unfortunately shows, only too easy
to misunderstand the link between faith and
intelligence and to create unconsciously an
hiatus, a dichotomy between the two, keeping
them in hermetically sealed compartments. One
result is that while one develops physically and
psychologically through adolescence into adult-
hood, the Faith can remain a blind loyalty or a
moral code or, much worse, just a jumble of in-
hibitions and taboos left over from the indoctrina-
tion period of early childhood.

Interesting to note here again that the vocabulary Paul uses here—in particular the opposition
between the mature adult (*teleios*) and the babe
(*nepios*)—was current in the Mysteries and neo-
Pythagorean schools. Both also spoke of feeding
milk to beginners and the uninitiated and solid
food, strong red meat, to the mature initiates,
and the more mature the stronger the meat. While
it would seem entirely natural for Paul to borrow
terminology of this kind, familiar to some of his

[1] 5.11–14.

hearers at least, we have to be careful to test the conclusions which some scholars have tried to draw from such premises. Thus it does not seem feasible to infer from the fact that Epictetus and others distinguished two classes of philosophers, the perfect (*teleioi*) and the deficient (*idiotai*), that such a distinction was in force in the Corinthian assembly, merely on the grounds that Paul refers somewhat obscurely to a class of *idiotai*.[1] But there is no doubt that he regarded it as highly desirable that they use their minds as well as their hearts to penetrate more deeply into the Christian mystery.

From what has been said so far apropos Paul's moral advice and instruction to these Christians of the first hour it might all appear rather remote and up in the air. It would certainly be a pity if such an impression were left, for if anything characterizes Paul's moral teaching it is its realism. When answering questions he is conscious all the time that he is dealing with people living in circumstances as complex as they are difficult and within the social and psychological pressures of a world which is only too real. Here again we find the antithesis with casuist morality, since this mentality cannot conceive of a person living in a

[1] 14.23. The basic sense of the word is "private", "without any public function", "not initiated"; here, it probably refers to any who were strangers to the habits of the Corinthian Christians.

precise moment of history, both social and personal, and subjected to pressures which are dynamically interactive.

This would be illustrated by the case of a typical convert living at that time in Corinth in an almost entirely unfriendly and unpropitious milieu. We can easily imagine some of the difficulties he would have if we have read the letter: What kind of food could he eat? Could he buy from butchers who stocked up with meat left over from pagan sacrifices? Would it be wise for him to make friends with pagan neighbours? Could he exchange visits? Could he take public office? Paul's attitude to this type of situation is highly instructive. His radical intuition into the absolute newness of the Christian reality enabled him to short-cut many of these problems. The old order which bred them had been left behind with the carefully wrapped cerements of death in the empty tomb on Easter morning. But the Christian had to go on living in the world:

> I wrote to you in my letter not to associate with immoral men; but I did not mean the immoral men of this world, or the greedy and robbers, or idolaters, since then you would need to go out of the world. [5.9–10.]

It is this reconciliation of the given facts of a situation with the Christian principle that is a sure hallmark of maturity, especially for those who, being in authority, dispose in some way of the lives of those within their jurisdiction. Here as elsewhere Paul is an example which can be proposed without reserve.

Paul's moral realism is never really hard to believe. His way of thinking and of speaking is, somehow, much in line with our own time. There are several reasons for this. Perhaps the greatest single change which has interposed between the language of revelation in the New Testament (much more so in the Old) and our own thought-patterns is that from an agrarian to an urban way of life; this is not just a social and economic change but has entailed a vast sociological and spiritual dislocation. Religion for thousands of years had spoken the language of an agrarian society, of men working the earth; it had its corn gods and its storm gods, and though Christianity transcended these religions, and indeed religion as such, the same kind of language and the same thought-patterns survived. Suffice it to think of the parables, the basic metaphors for the Kingdom, the saying about the grain of wheat that dies. With the Hellenistic missions, and especially those led by Paul, Christianity moved into the towns and found its first converts there. If it was to be understood it had to speak their language. That it did so is all to our gain and can be shown even in apparently insignificant ways:

Do you not know that in a race all the runners compete but only one receives the prize? So run that you may obtain it. Every athlete exercises self-control in all things. They do it to receive a perishable wreath, but we an imperishable. Well, I do not run aimlessly, I do not box as one beating the air; but I pommel my body and subdue it, lest after preaching to others I myself should be disqualified. [9.24–7.][1]

This is true missionary language, revolutionary at that time; there was no chance of misunderstanding for even the least sophisticated of Paul's congregation even if, which was improbable, he had never seen the Isthmian Games.

One cannot, however, speak of moral realism without coming to grips with the problem of conscience, since any realistic appraisal has to leave room for the individual conscience. This has been defined in many ways: the cynic has spoken of that part of us which feels rotten while the rest feels fine; others have thought of it as "the still, small voice", a kind of built-in sin-detector which works automatically. For the moral theologian it consists in a judgement of the practical reason,

---

[1] This short passage is full of technical terms taken from racing and boxing, e.g., *brabeion*, "the prize", *stephanos*, "the winner's wreath", *hypopiazo*, lit., "to hit beneath the eyes", *adokimos*, " disqualified" etc.

but this definition is purely functional. *Syneidesis*, "conscience", the word used by Paul, and by the Stoics, who had a highly developed teaching on the subject, means in the first place reflexive knowledge, the type which is peculiar to man; it refers generically to the kind of general awareness which a normal man has—his consciousness of his environment, of moral values, of the transcendental forces and dimensions of existence, and so on. This already gives us a valuable insight, since it shows moral conscience as, from the psychological point of view, part of man's general consciousness and therefore the product of an individual and unique history, influenced by his own attitudes and secret currents and cross-currents, and therefore with its area determined partially or entirely in advance to a certain pattern of action and thought. The education of conscience, the ability to make one's moral effort where it will be to best effect, is the work of a lifetime and therefore part of the individual's overall maturation and should not be considered in isolation. Once again we come up against the irrelevance of the casuistic approach which tends in practice to leave little room for this incommunicable element and wants to have everything sorted out in advance.

Paul insists throughout on the absolute priority of the claim of conscience and the need to direct it away from the immature states of compulsive fear and inhibition towards the life of free service in Christ, a movement, in short, towards interiority and freedom. For this it is absolutely necessary to have *knowledge* (this is Paul's term) —what we should call an instructed conscience. Take the case of legal and illegal food. The instructed Christian knows that the gods to whom the food is offered before going into the city *makella* are products of the imagination, so it makes no difference whether he eats or not:

> Food will not commend us to God. We are no worse off if we do not eat, and no better off if we do. [8.8.]

More than this, the freedom of the Christian's conscience should not, as a matter of principle, be determined by the scruples and misgivings of others:

> If one of the unbelievers invites you to dinner and you are disposed to go, eat whatever is set before you without raising any question on the ground of conscience. But if some one says to you: "This has been offered in sacrifice," then out of consideration for the man who informed you and for conscience' sake—I mean his conscience, not yours—do not eat it. For why should my liberty be determined by another man's scruples? [10.27–9.]

I am not only *free* to follow my conscience; I *must* be true to it, because that is the only way I know of being true to my innermost nature. No-one can dictate to my conscience or propose for my guidance a rule higher than my conscience— much less use it as a stick to beat me with by using different kinds of moral pressure. But here, too, there appears the Christian paradox, for if I desire liberty I must also be prepared to accept responsibility; I cannot have the one without the other. There is no possibility of "passing the buck", of getting other people, or much less a system automatically applied, to make my decisions for me. It must seem strange, when we read on every page Paul's insistence that the Church is a commonwealth of free men, how often this view has been abandoned in practice and indeed, to a mercifully reduced extent, still is. The call to faith is an invitation, the call to the religious life is also a free invitation; indeed, no action can be completely moral or even completely human unless it is free.

There is, however, a point of great importance to note here which emerges in the words of Paul just quoted, where he speaks of the other man's conscience. My conscience is, in a certain real sense, autonomous, but since I am a Christian it can only operate within the great context of charity if it is not to become merely an expression of my selfhood. Earlier on, this is stated more explicitly:

> Take care lest this liberty of yours somehow become a stumbling-block to the weak. For if anyone sees you, a man of knowledge, at table in an idol's temple, might he not be encouraged, if his conscience is weak, to eat food offered to idols? And so, by your knowledge, this weak man is destroyed, the brother for whom Christ died. Thus, sinning against your brethren and wounding their conscience when it is weak, you sin against Christ. Therefore, if food is a cause of my brother's falling, I will never eat meat, lest I cause my brother to fall. [8.9–13.]

My conscience, therefore, comes under charity as it does under the judgement of God, now that the blood of Christ has purified it from dead works to serve the living God.[1] And just as any living in society implies, in different degrees, an abdication of selfhood, much more so for the Christian, citizen of the divine commonwealth, the ultimate consideration is for the neighbour, "the brother for whom Christ died".

It is a strange irony, one of many which current interpretations of the Christian fact have provided at different moments of history, that the very same legalist, dead-letter system which Paul constantly

[1] Heb. 9.14.

urged his converts not to fall back into is so often proposed as the principal Christian ideal. This is a travesty, but its effects have been widely and deeply felt. One of these effects, which we can take as a last but typical example of this perversion of New-Testament teaching, is the idea of formation. As often used, the word connotes a preconceived pattern or form to which each person has to con-form. Since the form is the same for all, irrespective of background, personal history and temperament, there is envisaged only one ideal end-product. We have, therefore, an assembly-line production and should in all exactness speak of conformity rather than formation. It is interesting that Paul only once in his letters uses the verb "to form" and characteristically, he thinks of the metaphor of the living embryo, its development towards its own rich, full individuality:

> My little children, with whom I am again in travail until Christ be formed in you![1]

This formation of the Christ-life, the work of an entire lifetime, has to be the aim of all our moral efforts.

[1] Gal. 4.19.

The body is not meant for immorality but for the
    Lord
And the Lord for the body.
God raised the Lord
And will also raise us up by his power.

Man is the image and glory of God
But woman is the glory of man . . .
Woman is not independent of man
Nor man of woman;
For as woman was made from man
So man is now born of woman.

Shun immorality
Every other sin which a man commits is outside
    the body
But the immoral man sins against his own body
Do you not know that your body is a temple of
    the Holy Spirit?

Just as we have borne the image of the man of
    dust
So shall we also bear the image of the man of
    heaven.

THE REDEEMED BODY

WITHIN the moral field which we have been discussing what place has to be given to sexual morality? In view of the particular circumstances in which the letter was written this is an important question which can hardly be avoided. The reader is bound to be struck by the amount of space given to the discussion and solution of difficulties of this kind, so much so that he might be tempted to get a one-sided view. It is well known how, for a certain mentality, such discussion tends to fill the whole horizon, thus making the Sixth and Ninth in practice the First and Second Commandments. In fact, we could say that the ability to maintain perspective and proportion in this matter is one of the touchstones of maturity and rectitude of judgement in any period. It is interesting, for example, with what sureness of touch St Thomas categorizes sexual sin and how Dante, who followed his teaching and general scheme, places those who sin through unchastity in the second of the nine descending circles of his *Inferno*. In our own day, there is quite a volume of complaint that the kind of instruction given, the attitude taken up and inculcated is so often negative, frustrating and restrictive, as if the sexual appetite could in no way serve the divine purpose.[1] In view of this situation, it is possible that a reading of this letter, undertaken as part of the return upstream to the sources of our Christian life, might go some way towards correcting false perspectives and lead us to a positive appraisal of this basic aspect of our human existence.

There is, however, one fairly basic theological question which needs airing before we come to the letter itself. The way in which people think of this area of moral action is always, at least unconsciously, linked with their view of the body and how they understand it as a part or function of personality as a whole. The great example is the history of dualism and the sexual ethic which some dualist sects professed. It is disconcerting, when we stop to think of it, to what an extent we are still unconsciously influenced by this dualist way of thinking, as for example when we speak,

[1] See remarks in G. Gilleman, S.J., *The Primacy of Charity in Moral Theology*, London, Burns and Oates (1959), and summary in article in *Theology Digest*, 2 (1954): "Chastity introduces charity into the realm of sexual appetite so that this powerful instinct, far from opposing spiritual union with God and man, is made to serve it." (p. 18.)

with the Catechism, of the likeness to God being rather in the soul than in the body, or use some expressions of ascetical writers which are really more in keeping with Plato and Plotinus than John and Paul. Dualism sees the body either as evil or as of no account, whereas the Christian view sees it as part of our permanent and indestructible personality, a function or dynamism of one indivisible unity. We do not have a body, we *are* a body, and the whole point of our human mode of existence is that it is existence as body. It is precisely because a Christian anthropology faces this fact squarely and resists the temptation to speak of man as a soul unfortunately and temporarily walled up in a body that the Christian is able to come to grips, better than any other, with the real problems which this kind of existence brings to the surface. This, incidentally, goes some way to explaining Paul's realism in this field of morality.

Putting it more precisely, there are three Christian doctrines which bear directly upon a theology of the body and which differentiate Christianity most sharply from dualism or gnosticism, which has at all times been the greatest rival of Christianity: creation, the Incarnation, the resurrection of the body. Revelation teaches that *all* reality, including physical reality and therefore the body, comes from God and is good. Man is in the divine image; and this similarity is seen by the inspired author of the creation account in man as such, not just in his soul as abstracting from his body. If we read the story of our first parents with sympathy and insight we shall see, moreover, that the being like to God, the possession of an insight and power which was in some way divine, is shown particularly in the climax of the story with the begetting of offspring. The ability to create beings in his own image and to his likeness is represented as the area of man's greatest self-realization but also potentially his greatest failure. But all the time the lesson is driven home that the generative and reproductive powers are good and within the radius of the divine will—so much so that the Promise—to the first man, to Abraham, in the Sinai Covenant, to David—can be fulfilled only through the ordinary course of human generation. For the last editors of the Old Testament, in fact, generation, schematized in the form of genealogy, is identical with history.[1]

Considered from this viewpoint, there is a deep analogy between creation and incarnation. Both bring into existence a new reality, both proceed along the same line, the *mirabiliter* of the first followed by the *mirabilius* of the second; this can be taken as the starting-point for our understanding the relationship between the two covenants, as the spiritual exegesis of the Fathers shows.

[1] The Hebrew *toldot* means both "generations" and "history".

Both are attacked at their root by the dualist philosophy and world-view, and it was precisely to counter this that the whole structure of incarnation theology as we have it came into existence. This explains the insistence of New-Testament writers on the radical corporality, physicality, of Jesus, and the fact of his human generation:

> ... who was descended from David according to the flesh[1] ... that which was from the beginning, which we have heard, which we have seen with our eyes, which we have looked upon and touched with our hands ...[2]

The further Christianity developed, the more pervasive became the gnostic menace and the greater the insistence on the reality of the body of Christ; this can be seen as an urgent problem in the Pastorals and became even more marked in the immediate sub-apostolic period, particularly in Ignatius of Antioch:

> ... Jesus Christ, who was of the race of David, of Mary, who was truly born, who ate and drank, who truly suffered persecution under Pontius Pilate, who was truly crucified and died ... and who was truly raised from the dead, his Father raising him.[3]

[1] Rom. 1.3.
[2] 1 John 1.1.
[3] *Ad Trallianos*, 9, 1. *Alethos*, "truly", occurs four times in this short passage.

This can also be seen, if from a different angle, in the genealogies with which Matthew and Luke preface Christ's ministry, while in the Fourth Gospel it is built into a powerful incarnational theology summarized in the formula: "The Word became flesh."

It is, however, with the Resurrection that we come to the heart of the difficulty, as far as this letter is concerned. Our credal formula speaks of "the resurrection of the body" (eleventh article) whereas Paul, as a rule, more in accord with biblical terminology, refers to the resurrection from the dead.[1] This mystery, the risen body of Christ as an anticipation of the general resurrection, stands at the centre of all Paul's thinking. In this living presence and new reality the final reality is already present. By contact with it one passes from the sphere of the carnal to the spiritual and so there is already set in motion the process and movement towards what we are to be when we shall be reconstituted as a spiritual being, but also as *body*, though in a way of which we can now have only a vague and analogous idea. What is certain is that the body is deeply involved in this creative process of renewal, right from the moment of baptism onward, and that con-

[1] Hebrew has a word for "flesh", "living person", "corpse", but none for "body" as distinct from "soul".

sequently a purely naturalistic sexual ethic is out
of the question:

> "Food is meant for the stomach and the
> stomach for food"—and God will destroy both
> one and the other. The body is not meant for
> immorality, but for the Lord, and the Lord for
> the body. And God raised the Lord and will
> also raise us up by his power. [6.13–14.]

The point of Paul's reply to this specious *apologia*
for promiscuity is obvious: what he refers to elsewhere as "the redemption of our bodies"[1] has
already begun with our incorporation into Christ
and sacramental contact with him. The sexual
function is not in the same line as the digestive—
it is not just like eating and drinking, with no
further implications. Sexuality is not an extra,
for man's and woman's total being is radically
sexual. There can be no union without a total
commitment, a "becoming one flesh". This fulfilment in the flesh, which goes to the centre of
affectivity and existence as body, must fall under
the consecration of the person implied in baptism
and life *in Christ*. This consecration is fulfilled
only in the resurrection, and it is obvious from
Paul's experience at Athens and at Corinth
(ch. 15) that for these Greeks this was a major
stumbling-block.

[1] Rom. 8.23.

These general theological principles take on flesh and blood and a sense of immediacy with a reading of how Paul handles concrete cases of conscience which come up. There were quite a number which dealt with questions of this kind, as might be expected from the milieu. In fact, of ten types of mortal sinners which he lists (those who cannot enter the Kingdom of God) four, and possibly five, are guilty of sexual sin.[1] The reason for this selection becomes clear when he goes on to state, in a tone of surprising candour, that it was just these sins of which so many of them had been guilty in their old pre-baptismal existence, the potent, seductive smell of which still hung around even after baptism.

This, therefore, is an example of Paul's pastoral concern, not of a morbid preoccupation with sexual aberration. It was not just that such aberration, both natural and unnatural, was common and notorious at Corinth, as it was indeed in the rest of that world—a fact which will be obvious to anyone with only a superficial acquaintance with the Classics; what was more dangerous and

---

[1] 6.9–11. It may be that *idolators* refers indirectly to sexual sin connected with pagan cult, bearing in mind both the scriptural use of the word in this sense and the situation at Corinth. We could compare Gal. 5.19, where there is another such list with sexual sins mentioned first. In the list of sins in Rom. 1.28 they are, however, almost completely absent, since Paul had dealt with this subject at length in the preceding verses.

insidious was that prominent philosophers and thinkers wrote widely publicized *apologiae* for such conduct—prostitution and homosexuality in particular. This must have left many spirits troubled and confused. The line of argument usually taken, familiar at Corinth even among Christians, was the old one that *naturalia non sunt turpia*; you can't go wrong if you follow nature; it's all right so long as you don't hurt anyone. Since this is still the standard approach, and since it still impresses some Christians with its appearance of fairness and rationality, it might be a good idea to take a closer look at the way in which Paul answers this objection.

What he stresses first of all is something which is often forgotten, namely, that sexual activity is of its nature ordered to life in society, to otherness, living together. It is *the* example, right at the roots of our experience, of our need one for the other, since it cannot reach its proper end in isolation. Already, therefore, it contains the idea of community. All sexual activity comes under this basic orientation, which has to be borne in mind in making a moral judgement on such acts, whether carried out alone or with the co-operation of others. Another way of putting this is by saying that chastity must always be considered within charity.

But already, on the natural level, sexual activity contains the seeds of a greater and inclusive

7

mystery. In the Old Testament, the Yahwist brings his account of how life first started in our world to a climax with the creation of woman. What this account expresses, in pictorial form, is that woman comes from near man's heart, that she needs man as he needs her and that they find their completion in one another. This union of two in one flesh is already full of mystery and promise. We could, perhaps, gauge the depth and originality of this presentation by comparing it with Plato's account of the origins and nature of sexual activity in the *Symposium*. Here, in order to give some explanation of how man's division, and the pain and frustration it causes, first started, the philosopher is forced outside the world of experience and conceives of a primitive hermaphroditic being who is divided in two, thus giving Man and Woman, and who will eventually be reunited.[1] Unity is thus achieved, but at the expense of personal identity; the balance is upset and the mystery within this most intimate and baffling field of human relationship is not faced. For Plato the man-woman relationship is essentially disorder and all heterosexual activity basically inimical to man's true interests. This is completely contrary to the Christian view.

[1] This idea has profoundly influenced gnostic writings and can be seen in the way the Nag Hammadi texts (the so-called Gospel of Thomas) twist certain Gospel sayings.

According to this, the man-woman relationship is consecrated by sacramental contact with Christ, as we have seen in dealing with the sacrament of matrimony, and this is to be understood as within the wider sacramental consecration of nature and the movement within nature towards unity and completion. In this is seen clearly the social aspect of the sacraments and how the union of man with woman is, in the deepest sense, a figure of the union of Christ with the Church—what Paul elsewhere calls "a great mystery".[1] Here, too, is implied the same thing if expressed more indirectly. When warning them against promiscuity and the frequentation of prostitutes he reminds them:

Do you not know that your bodies are members of Christ? [6.15.]

and a little later:

Do you not know that your body is a temple of the Holy Spirit within you? [6.19.]

It is not just by accident that Paul here, in speaking to the individual Christian on this subject, echoes what he has already said to the Christian Church at Corinth collectively in dealing with the need for unity:

Do you not know that you are God's temple

[1] Eph. 5.32.

and that the Spirit of God dwells in you?
[3.16.]

This means that the former is much more than a
pious aphorism, however striking; such conduct
was unthinkable because of their belonging to
Christ through a prior claim staked in baptism
and through their belonging to him and to their
fellow Christians in the Church. Through this
societas sanctorum they are taken into the *societas
Dei*, into the intimate life of the Trinity, that is,
into ultimate reality, where alone the tension
between union and personal identity, the social
and the individual, is resolved.

These principles governing life in the Church
are applied straight away in the first case which
comes up for solution in the letter—the sad affair
of a Christian guilty of incest. (5.1.) In command-
ing them to shun this unrepentant public sinner,
to treat him, at least for the time being, as *excom-
municatus vitandus*, he uses the metaphor of the
bit of yeast in the flour which permeates the whole
mass—probably with the Gospel parable in mind.
This leads on to the Passover, which was probably
then imminent, and the practice of "casting out"
any remnants of leavened bread which might be
about the house before the opening of the great
feast. This served as a telling expression of the
newness of the life which opens with baptism,
especially in view of the close connection of

Christian initiation with the celebration of the Christian Passover. In the same way, when speaking of the sins which exclude from the Kingdom, he sees them as unthinkable in view of this new life which begins with baptism; the words which he uses here are in fact nothing but synonyms for baptism:

> ... but you have been *cleansed*, but you have been *sanctified*, but you have been *justified* in the name of the Lord Jesus Christ, and in the Spirit of our God. [6.11.]

We should note carefully this immediate, instinctive recourse, when dealing with moral problems, to this new life in Christ. We who are continually being challenged to provide reasons for the traditional teaching on chastity or against practices such as extramarital intercourse, the use of artificial means to control reproduction and the like, so often find ourselves on the terrain of natural law and applied reason that we too easily forget or underplay the context of the Christian life and the spiritual perspectives of the enquirer or questioner, so decisive in this kind of dialogue. For Paul, all men are either "in the flesh" or "in the Spirit" and the perspectives of both are bound to be profoundly different. We find another example of the same thing in the instinctive recourse not to legal minimism (as so often happens with us) but to the principle of Christian liberty when Paul goes on to exhort his Christians to avoid fornication. He takes up the slogan of those who had, probably with premeditation, distorted his teaching on liberty—"All things are lawful" (6.12)—and uses it in his own way to show how "free love" is neither an expression of nor a means to real freedom—it's not so easy as that!

"All things are lawful for me"—but not all things are profitable. "All things are lawful for me" but I do not intend to be enslaved by anything. [6.12.]

It is true that some commentators have seen this as a Stoic dictum, but there is a world of difference between the Stoic *apathia*, the goal of insensibility to passion, and Paul's idea of a Christian striving to be free, but free in the centre of life lived in the body.[1]

In the section of the letter which follows this exhortation we have another opportunity of studying Paul's pastoral concern. In that city of Aphrodite, Goddess of Love, he had to preach a high ideal of chastity to people of all conditions from slaves and menials to intellectuals and well-to-do traders. It might be asked whether he did really deal with these personal sexual problems with the realism which the situation demanded.

---

[1] Compare the Stoic saying: "Mihi res, non me rebus, submittere conor." See Allo, *Première Épître aux Corinthiens*, p. 142.

He foresaw some of the difficulties, but there is nothing on some aspects which are uppermost in people's minds today, for example, that of family regulation. Here something is asked of *us* more than of Paul, who was under no obligation to go into what would be for us interesting questions of social history. For a society which accepted and condoned abortion and the suppression of unwanted offspring and in which the frequentation of prostitutes was socially acceptable, family limitation was no problem. And then for all, including Christians, we have to bear in mind that there was a considerably shorter life expectation and, within this shorter span, a lower fertility index than is general today. Thus it is not surprising that no query of this kind features among the *casus* put to him here for solution.

With Paul's attitude to marriage we have already dealt in the chapter on the sacraments. One hears frequent references to his unsympathetic approach to the richness and fulfilment which can be found in physical intimacy when raised to the status of a sacrament. Some trace this to the fact that he himself was single—a fact which is certain despite outdated controversy on one or two texts in other letters[1]—or to some

[1] The offending texts are 1 Cor. 9.5 and Phil. 4.3 which Revised Standard Version translates "true yokefellow" and the New English Bible "my loyal comrade". The difficulty for this view is of course Paul's statement in 1 Cor. 7.7.

supposed and purely hypothetical experience of his early years, or to a leaning towards a false spiritualism later found in the Encratic sects. What, however, we have to look into here is the situation of the anonymous interlocutor rather than that of Paul, and nowhere more so than in the thorny chapter where the question of sexual abstention and virginity arises, a question which has been the source of so much misunderstanding.

The introductory phrase should warn us at once that Paul is concerned with answering a particular query, since this is the usual way such an answer begins:

Concerning the points you mentioned . . . [7.1.]

The first of these points evidently dealt with the married state in the light of the overwhelming awareness of the Lord's coming. Should the unmarried go into marriage just the same? Should the married continue as before in the exercise of their rights? Here we come straightaway to the centre of the misunderstanding on the Christian attitude to virginity. Both in the Jewish and pagan world this practice, if not quite unknown, had little meaning. The rabbis, taking the command to increase and multiply[1] literally and distributively, imposed marriage and the raising of a family as a sacred duty. Gradually, however, with the inten-

[1] Gen. 1.28.

sification of the messianic expectation, the anxious scanning of the horizon for signs of the final catastrophe, the idea matured in some Jewish circles that, since marriage is connected directly with the survival and destiny of the human race, it could hardly play a part in the latter days. A valuable precedent existed in the career of Jeremiah, who was ordered by God to remain celibate, as a living sign of the imminent end of the Chosen People in their own land.[1] One example of how this eschatological thinking bore on the question of marriage and virginity can be studied in the Qumran community, in which celibacy was practised, at least for a time, in a clear eschatological context. Sexual abstention had been, right from the beginning, a rule in the Holy War, and it is well known how these Essene monks conceived of the last days as crowned by a "War of the Sons of Light against the Sons of Darkness". How far this idea had spread it is impossible to say, but it seems clear that where it existed it was in function of the last age.

Turning to the mysterious Gospel saying on marriage and celibacy, we find a strong confirmation of this view. We note first of all in the context[2] that Jesus makes demands upon his followers in a way similar to, but more radical than, that of the Essenes. In fact, in respect both of chastity and

[1] Jer. 16.1–4.
[2] Matt. 19.

poverty, Jesus states plainly the difficulties involved and, by implication, the special grace required. Paul also describes this as a "charism" or grace. (7.7.) In regard to the third class of "eunuchs", those, that is, who practise voluntary chastity, we are told that this is "on account of the Kingdom of Heaven"—a clearly eschatological term referring to the rule of God to be established at the end of time. In short, Christian virginity has to be seen in the context of the history of salvation, not in the framework of a particular philosophy or anthropology. If we go on to ask, with the deepest sense of reverence, why Jesus himself chose this way which he here explains to his disciples, it is surely in the last analysis because Jesus is himself *the* eschatological event, the Kingdom of God present to us, the final self-manifestation of God in flesh and blood and history.

We can be certain that Paul had pondered on these verses of the Gospel—even though it is likely that they reached their present state only after the writing of this letter. It is important to bear this in mind in order to avoid misunderstanding what he is saying, in particular when he insists so much on what may seem a negative approach to marriage, namely, as a safeguard against the uprising tide of concupiscence. We must also bear in mind the overcharged atmosphere of expectation at Corinth and elsewhere in the early days, which, as we have seen, bore directly on the question of a state in life, in a way which would afterwards be somewhat modified. This expectation comes through clearly and urgently in a well-known passage where Paul warns, almost in a whisper, that the time is running out:

The appointed time has grown very short; from now on, let those who have wives live as though they had none, and those who mourn as though they were not mourning, and those who rejoice as though they were not rejoicing, and those who buy as though they had no goods, and those who deal with the world as though they had no dealings with it. For the form of this world is passing away. [7.29-31.]

Within the total content of revelation we can now see the Christian life as eschatological primarily in its very nature and ontology rather than in any temporal sense, and therefore it would be unwise to start drawing conclusions from these verses without bearing in mind the particular situation in which and on account of which they were written. Paul was too much of a realist to neglect the situation and the needs of the normal man, the *chrétien moyen sensuel*, as we can see in his insistence, against the extremists, that no-one should risk breaking up a marriage by unilateral action. As an example of how far the purely temporal expectation faded into the background we can read how Paul, writing at a later stage to Timothy, positively encourages the young to get married and raise a family.[1]

For anyone looking for a treatise on the body and its function in the Christian life or a consideration of *eros* in its relation to *agape*, in the manner of some modern studies, or a great prophetic statement on human love and its place in the supernatural vocation of mankind, as in some of the prophets of the Old Dispensation, First Corinthians is bound to be somewhat disappointing. But if Paul could not and did not attempt to say the last word, he at least grasped the nettle of commitment firmly; he did not politely ignore the problems which sexual behaviour brought to the surface or foist his people off with discrete generalities, or make the mistake of preaching anaemia as a virtue. Out of the apparently unpromising raw material at hand we can watch him at work trying to bring into existence the new man in Christ in and through a progress towards liberty and fulfilment on the human level. To the married his word is that their state was not an unfortunate necessity or a poor second best but a basic means of fulfilling themselves in each other; to the celibate, that theirs was not one to take refuge in or drift into, but

[1] 1 Tim. 5.14. Cf. his advice to bishops (3.2) and deacons (3.12).

had to be the result of a positive choice, an imitation of Christ which made possible, ideally, a more inclusive and outgoing love for others. It could have been so easy for Paul, with his high ideals and horror of impurity, to have turned his back on that fast and loose city and gone on further afield; but we read that he had a vision of the Lord at night, probably soon after he arrived at Corinth and when in the depths of discouragement, who said to him:

> Fear not, but speak and do not be silent; for I am with you and no-one will lay hands on you to do you harm, for I have many people in this city.[1]

It was in union with that sympathy and that purpose of bringing into existence the people of God that Paul worked for the eighteen months that followed.

[1] Acts 18.9–10.

I will pray with the Spirit
And I will pray with the mind also;
I will sing with the Spirit
And I will sing with the mind also.

Our Lord, come!

There is one God the Father
From whom are all things and for whom we exist
And one Lord Jesus Christ
Through whom are all things and through whom
*   we exist.*

No-one can say: "Jesus is the Lord"
Except by the Holy Spirit.

LITURGY AND LIFE

For the increasing number of people who are beginning to look in the direction in which the Church is moving in our time it is becoming more and more obvious that what is basic to all the movement of reform is the need to create the conditions in which it will be possible to *see* the Church as a community, as the assembly of the People of God. Modern subjectivism has driven this social consciousness underground, as can be seen in the preponderance of certain devotional attitudes; and this devotional subjectivism is carried over into *the* Christian assembly, the Sunday Mass, where it is still all too easy for each one to exist as a separate devotional enclave and for the prayers of the worshippers present to go up to God in vertical and parallel lines which never meet.

What can we learn from our reading of 1 Corinthians to help us to enter into the meaning and spirit of Christian liturgy and correct our outlook accordingly? We are not going to be concerned with the external conduct of services, questions of time and place and the like, though this letter tells us quite a lot about these things.[1] Nor shall we spend any time trying to define what we mean by "liturgy" and the difference between liturgical and non-liturgical or para-liturgical acts—at least, not directly. It is a striking demonstration of the extent to which the old Jewish liturgical order had been completely superseded by the Christ-event that, leaving aside a special usage in the Letter to the Hebrews, to which we shall return, the very word *leitourgia* and its derivatives occur only nine times in the New Testament, twice in Luke and seven times in the Pauline corpus, but not at all in this letter.

What we do want to look for is the spirit and

[1] The Lord's Supper of which Paul speaks in ch. 11 was certainly on the Lord's Day (16.2); it might be reasonably surmised that it was held in the house of Stephanas (16.15). As regards structure, we learn little from Paul's letters, and comparisons with the synagogue service are very speculative. See Delling, *Worship in the New Testament*, London (1962), pp. 43–6 (though the English translation can hardly be recommended). In 1 Cor. we hear of instruction (14.19), of the use of hymns (14.15,26) and of various liturgical formulae— e.g., *Maranatha* (16.22), *Amen* (14.16; cf. a magnificent passage in 2 Cor. 1.17–20). We might also deduce from the letter the use of doxologies, trinitarian forms (e.g., 12.4–6, cf. Eph. 1.11–13), blessings and thanksgivings (1.4; 15.57) and expressions of praise. In ch. 11 we hear of the eucharistic assembly and in ch. 14 of the problem of spontaneity and order. We might mention too the kiss of peace (16.20) and the collection (16.1–2).

the meaning of liturgical action, the secret but powerful links which connect the Christian liturgy to life lived in the world and in the Church. This means that we start from the actual service, the plenary gathering together of all the Christians of a local Church in a certain place and at a certain time. It is already of great significance—we have already seen this point—that this is referred to by Paul as the *ekklesia*, the same term as that used for the Church as an abstract reality. Thus, when he addresses his letter "to the Church of God which is in Corinth" (1.2) he is thinking of that particular community gathered together for worship, during which meeting the letter would have been read, just as certain Scripture passages are read in our liturgical meetings. That Paul actually thought in this way and had this intention can be confirmed by noting the at times very strong liturgical flavour of many of the expressions used in his letters to the Churches, for example, when he refers to them as "they who call upon the name of Jesus Christ our Lord" (1.2) or begins with a solemn thanksgiving prayer (1.4).[1] The "schisms" which he laments as breaking up the unity of the Corinthian Church (1.11) are reflected exactly in the "schisms" threatening the unity and very existence of the weekly meeting of the "Church" (11.18). This means that their abstract identity as

[1] Especially if, as Lietzmann maintains, 1.2 is parallel to a Jewish liturgical formula. See Delling, p. 49, *n*. 4.

a group is actualized and made concrete only when they come together *in unum* (11.20), as a "Church".[1] This way of thinking, so simple and yet so momentous in its implications, springs doubtless from the Hebrew and Jewish idea of corporate identity realized in the actual here-and-now community, as can be seen from the Old-Testament use of the term *kol Israel* ("all Israel") as expressing their sense of corporate solidarity in and through the plenary assembly of the tribes. Thus the Christian assembly, wherever and at whatever time it is realized, is the local Church *in actu*, and the local Church is, in its turn, the actualization of the Great Church. The same term is used by Paul for all three stages.

Take, again, Paul's use of the term "fellowship" (*koinonia*). When he tells his Corinthians that they have been called into fellowship or communion with the Lord Jesus Christ (1.9) he means not just union of each of them distributively with Christ but a real communion—a union between each other and between the community and the present Lord. This bears directly, but in a way in which we are not perhaps accustomed to think of, upon our own Christian assembly. When we speak of Holy Communion we should think not just of a personal union with Christ whom we receive but of an intensification of the union among our-

[1] See also throughout ch. 14, where "the Church" refers to the assembly; *vv.* 5,12,19,23,28.

selves which the very fact of our having come together *in unum* should imply. Moreover, if we bear in mind the Lord's saying "Where there are two or three gathered together in my name, there I am in the midst of them", it should become apparent that the divine presence is connected with our own co-presence, one to the other, and that this is true in a particular way is the eucharistic assembly with the "Real Presence" in the sacrament. This divine presence in the Christian assembly is a fact, and it is surely one of the chief objects of our liturgical reform to enable it to be *experienced* by the community as a fact—not perhaps exactly in the way it was experienced as such in the Corinthian assembly and that of other Churches of the first hour, much less in that of the pentecostal Churches of a later age; but an outsider who might happen to wander in should, as Paul pointed out, be able to exclaim that "truly God is among you!" (14.25).

There are other ways in which we can view this primary fact of Christian existence as Paul understood it. For example, the excommunication of the immoral Christian (5.1ff) meant first and foremost that he was excluded from the community assembly, that he was no longer "in communion". This is clear from the way in which Paul enjoins on them to put into effect his command when they are gathered together with the power of the Lord Jesus Christ. (5.4.) From what follows it may even be that he has in mind the great Easter gathering of the Church. If we were to examine the various terms used for "Christian" in this letter we should find also that most if not all of them essentially describe the Christian as present in the plenary assembly. For example, the term "saints" (1.2) is applied to them not, of course, as ethically perfect, which they evidently were not, but as members of the holy assembly inspired by the Holy Spirit, an inspiration shown in the charismatic gifts.

In the same context he speaks of "those without" and "those within" (5.12–13) and later on, when condemning their misconduct at the community meal, he brings in the old opposition between the gathered Church or assembly and the world outside (11.32). Perhaps most striking of all in this respect is the use of the term "the Many" (*polloi*) with reference to the Christian community gathered together for the celebration of the Lord's Supper (10.17), for this expression is a literal, even too literal, translation of the Hebrew word *rabbim*, the Many, a technical term for an exclusive assembly, particularly in contemporary sectarian Judaism.[1] Thus the Christian

[1] See Mark 14.24 and parallels for words of institution. For the use of the term at Qumran for the Community see F. Moore Cross Jnr, *The Ancient Library of Qumran*, 2nd ed., Doubleday (1961), p. 231. It might be added that "excommunication" at Qumran implied first and foremost exclusion from the Meal.

assembly expresses the unity of the Church as such both in its internal cohesion and in the preservation of its identity *vis-à-vis* the world.

In the light of this strongly emphasized theology of the local worshipping community it is highly interesting how the emphasis has, in recent discussions of the nature of the Church, shifted from the concept of the Mystical Body, one which, though not explicitly scriptural, has given valuable insights, to that of the People of God. This is a direct result of a deepened study of St Paul's teaching on the Church which has brought to light that the figure of the body, while often recurring and full of meaning, is not the most basic to his way of thinking, taken as it is from Greek sociology and not from the Scriptures, as is the figure of a Chosen People.

A direct and even obvious corollary of this community theology is that *all* are involved in the liturgical meeting. From our reading of this letter we should have gathered that the assemblies at Corinth must have been rather lively affairs. The account of the community meal which ended with the Lord's Supper seems more like a parish social which has got out of hand than our idea of a liturgical function. (11.17ff.) Similarly, the exercise of the ecstatic gifts (14.1ff) must have been nearer to some primitive pentecostal groups than anything else. This involvement of the whole worshipping community is basic to our understanding of what the eucharistic assembly or the Sunday Mass is, or even what liturgy of any kind is. The very word, which means "public task", points to a fact which is borne out by the history of religions in general; in early Greek ritual, for example, the sacred action in which all joined took place in the *orchestra* (the dancing floor) and only at a later stage, when ritual was passing into drama, was the *theatre*, the place for spectators, added. We note that Paul, in speaking of the essential eucharistic prayers and actions, uses the plural:

> The cup of blessing which we bless, is it not a participation in the blood of Christ? The bread which we break, is it not a participation in the body of Christ? Because there is one bread, we who are many are one body, for we all partake of the one bread. [10.16–17.][1]

A glance through the missal will show that the eucharistic prayers are all likewise, with the exception of the three prayers which the priest says privately as a personal preparation for Communion, fully expressive of an act which the community is performing. It is *they* who must, through the action, "announce the death of the Lord until he come". (11.26.)

---

[1] For different interpretations of the first person plural, see E. B. Allo, *Première Épître*, p. 238.

Here again, the starting-point of this idea, which ought to be obvious but is not, is the community at worship as the actualization of the People of God. Whatever polemical use may have been made of certain scriptural texts in the sixteenth century, it remains true that this people is described in the Old Testament as "a kingdom of priests, a holy nation",[1] a description taken up and developed in the New Testament, in what is possibly the context of a baptismal address.[2] Out of this ontologically holy (because chosen by God) and priestly people—the word means the same "laity"—one man is chosen and specially delegated to represent the rest in the eucharistic act; he prays and performs the action in their name and on their behalf. There is something which he alone can do, but his essential function is to recapitulate the priestly function of the community of which he is also a part. It is only in recent years that there has been among Catholics a decisive return to this biblical doctrine after the reaction against the Reformers' "priesthood of all believers" had run its natural course, just as it is only in comparatively recent times that the vernacular movement has gathered strength with the fading of the reaction against Protestant nationalism. Here we have, incidentally, an important example of the relation of liturgy to life,

[1] Exod. 19.6.
[2] 1 Pet. 2.4–9.

since the way in which the priest-people relationship within the liturgical act is understood reflects on this relationship outside of the Church service.

But we still have to discover what is the real link between what the Christian does in church and his everyday life out of church. It is not at all self-evident to the majority of Christians, unfortunately, that such a link does or should exist. For many a Catholic Mass-going is an obligation imposed by the Church, no doubt for very good reasons, a more or less isolated event on Sunday morning or perhaps Sunday evening. The priest says the Mass and he has to be present, under pain of venial sin as from the beginning, of mortal sin as from the Offertory. Perhaps he takes along a missal or rosary beads and tries to ward off distractions as best he can until he is told, in the *Ite Missa Est*, that it is time for him to leave, or nearly so. No doubt this description is not universally valid, but even for those who, in the face of considerable difficulties, have understood what it is all about, it will not always be clear how it is all related to the secular realities with which the rest of their waking hours are filled.

The answer will come for anyone reading this letter and feeling in every page the breath of the Holy Spirit. It is the presence of the Spirit which constitutes the Christian life and which is the soul of the life of the Church and of the individual Christian assembly. The Spirit is received in baptism and permeates the whole of baptized existence. For anyone who has experienced this even remotely all else is darkness and death. It is just this which has to overflow into the Christian liturgical assembly, giving it its particular character. This is clear from what Paul was to write a few years later from Corinth to the Roman Church:

> So then, brethren, we are debtors, not to the flesh, to live according to the flesh—for if you live according to the flesh you will die, but if by the Spirit you put to death the deeds of the body you will live. For all who are led by the Spirit of God are sons of God. For you did not receive the spirit of slavery to fall back into fear, but you have received the spirit of sonship. When we cry, "Abba! Father!" it is the Spirit himself bearing witness with our spirit that we are children of God.[1]

Notice the sequence: the Spirit is received in baptism—the baptized who lives according to the Spirit, not according to the old law of selfhood experiences this living and active presence—this flows over into prayer and worship. Worship is first and foremost a communion between the Holy Spirit and the worshipping and praying community—the verb is in the plural. This is all the more striking in that the retention of the original

[1] Rom. 8.12–16.

form *Abba* can be satisfactorily explained only on the grounds of liturgical usage, and we know that the Lord's Prayer was in use from ancient times in both the eucharistic service and the baptismal liturgy.[1]

As it is the Spirit who testifies in prayer, it is the presence of the Spirit which makes the liturgical assembly what it is. Without it we should have merely an aggregate of individuals, with the Spirit there is a corporate, organic unity; something more than the sum total of the parts. This lies behind Paul's assertion that the Corinthian Church is a temple in which the Spirit lives (3.16) and, to an even greater extent, behind the comparison with the human body (12.27). We miss the point of what Paul is trying to express in this latter instance if we think just of Aesop's fable and the interdependence of the various members of the body. The real point here is the existence in every part of the visible body of a mysterious, lifegiving reality which comes from beyond it, that reality which, though we cannot fully understand it, makes all the difference between a living person and a corpse. Here again we must not divide the sacramental from the social; just as the Real Presence must be taken with the co-presence of the worshipping members one to the other, so

---

[1] Cf. Gal. 4.6. A liturgical origin is strengthened by the use of the verb *krazo*, "cry", which has a definite liturgical background.

must the body of the Lord in the sacrament be taken with the assembled Church, which is the body of Christ, as Paul repeatedly insists.

Liturgical assemblies, then, and in particular the great eucharistic assembly, are meant to express and focus the whole of the Spirit—indwelt life of the local Christian community. For Paul's Christians, this was not just a truth apprehended in the mind, but something experienced. This gave rise to the free exercise of the Spirit-given gifts, in particular that of ecstatic prayer, in their meetings —which Paul discusses in ch. 12. There is no doubt that there was here a very marked human and natural element, a hangover from the orgiastic and ecstatic religion of which many of them had certainly had some experience before baptism. Paul states this explicitly (12.2), and was evidently much concerned with the balance between freedom and order. The thoughtful Christian of today, reading this letter, will doubtless see our problem as at the other end of the scale from that of the Corinthian Church. A gradual etiolation of the sense of Christian freedom in life has helped to produce a certain rigidity and formalism in the conduct of our liturgical services which make it often difficult for a congregation to experience, to *feel*, that the Spirit is indeed among them. No doubt liturgical reforms currently under discussion—a greater use of the vernacular, the gradual disappearance of adventitious elements in the service which now mean little, the increasing use of lay readers and the general redistribution of functions, all making for a clearer understanding of the basic structure of the Mass —will make a big difference in this respect.

This leads us on to a further stage in our attempt to understand what the liturgical service meant in those early days. It was a direct experience of the presence of the Holy Spirit at work in the community gathered together; indeed, the service *is* the work of the Spirit, since it is he who has brought them together and who prays in and through them. The most spectacular, and in some ways equivocal, sign of the Spirit's presence was seen in the charismatic and ecstatic gifts, especially what is usually called the Gift of Tongues. Now, if we turn to Luke's description of the first Pentecost we shall find the basic explanation not only of these gifts but of the very presence of the Spirit in early Christian liturgy. They were all gathered together *in unum*,[1] either in a private house or, as some think, in the Temple. They suddenly heard something *like* a mighty wind and saw something *like* fire—language typical of a numinous experience. They were filled with the Holy Spirit and the direct result was the speaking with tongues. Later on, we are told that this phenomenon made a great impression on those

[1] *Epi to auto*, Acts 2.1—"in one place". The same phrase is used in 1 Cor. 11.20.

who witnessed it, but that some took them to be
drunk (the Feast of Weeks was a time for cele-
brating); and it is interesting to note that Paul
too, in speaking of these ecstatic gifts as later in
use in the Corinthian Church, is worried lest anyone who happens to look in on them should come
to a similar conclusion.[1] Leaving aside the fact
that Luke, in writing up this account, had
certainly had experience of these Spirit-given gifts
in the Churches, perhaps in particular that of
Antioch,[2] what he is telling us is, in effect, that
right from the beginning the presence of the Spirit
is *the* characteristic of the age of the Church. This
comes out more clearly still with Peter's discourse,
in which he explains the strange sight which the
onlookers had seen as the fulfilment of the Old-
Testament prophecies of the last, the messianic
age. The quotation from Joel means that the
final age is the age of the Spirit and that is made
concrete, visible and actual in the Church. If we
follow the same line of reasoning as above, this in
its turn points to the actual liturgical gathering as
a realization of the gathered People of God of the
messianic age. Each individual receives the Spirit

[1] Acts 2.12–13; cf. 1 Cor. 14.23.
[2] Barnabas of that Church was "full of the Holy
Spirit" (Acts 11.24); there was the prophet Agabus (11.28)
and in 13.1 prophets and teachers, among them Saul,
are mentioned. It is remarkable how Luke's Gospel is so
full of Christian joy and the manifestations of the Spirit.

at baptism—this is clear from the way baptism is described in Acts, that of the Samaritan Christians or of Cornelius and his family, for example[1] —but he receives it as an initiation into the messianic people. The Pentecost event represents the baptism of the whole Christian community, upon which the Spirit comes in visible form as it did upon Jesus at his baptism. It is hardly an accident that Luke describes both these events as taking place in the course of prayer.[2] He brings out even more clearly the role of the Spirit in the liturgical life of the community in the incident related in Acts, sometimes referred to as the Little Pentecost, where the early Jerusalem community, in the course of public liturgical prayer, experienced once again a numinous intervention of the Spirit and were given a new lease of life which enabled them to exercise fully the great Christian prerogative of speaking freely and without fear.[3]

At this stage an objection will probably be made: You say that the Christian service is the embodiment of the Church as an eschatological community, as the community of the last age.

[1] Acts 8.15; 10.44–8.

[2] Luke 3.21; Acts 2.1 where the terms used imply a gathering for prayer.

[3] Acts 4.24–31; "with boldness" (31), literally "with *parresia*". This latter is a term rooted in the life of the Greek *polis* and refers to the right of every citizen to say everything he thinks fit without fear of the consequences.

But can we really believe this nowadays as Paul and his Christians seem to have done? Can we really be expected to believe that the earth is going to fail us at any minute and that the Lord's coming is just round the corner? And if not, how can *our* Christian service, and that means the Mass, really represent Christian existence in the last age?

Our Mass is a combination of two services, originally, as far as we can see, separate in time and place of celebration, the service of the word of God and the eucharistic service. The heart and soul of the first—the Mass of the Catechumenate —is the solemn reading of the Gospel passage. It does not necessarily deal with *the* event of salvation, the death and resurrection of the Lord, except during Holy Week; but everything in the Gospel is related to that event for the simple reason that everything which is in the Gospel is there because the writer saw it as relevant to the original message or *kerygma*. Thus a miracle story is there as a sign of the divine reality breaking into human existence, of God coming to us in Jesus. This first part, then, leads up to the celebration of the great saving act of the death of the Lord, which Paul describes as a *remembrance* service (11.24) and in which the whole community proclaims the death of the Lord until he come (11.26), but proclaims it *through* the action, through the eating and drinking. This means, incidentally, that the action itself must speak and be understood without the need of an interpreter or an explanatory manual. Through this action the community is brought into saving contact with the divine reality which is manifested in Jesus, which contact goes beyond time and space, since this divine reality is also the final reality, the *eschaton* present by anticipation. Thus the local community realizes in itself, through the service, the meaning of the Church as the community of the last age.

The movement of liturgical reform has as one of its most serious aims to make this truth stand out clearly within the structure of the service, in particular within the Great Prayer, which is throughout a prayer of thanksgiving addressed to the Father, concerned with the climax of salvation history.

The whole of the eucharistic action is poised so as to reveal the mystery of the Beyond in and through the mystery of our existence in time. It looks backward to an event in the past, it lives through the presence of the Spirit active within it, it looks forward with longing to the coming of the Lord and the final fulfilment; a threefold orientation which is expressed very well in the prayer *O Sacrum Convivium*. This attitude to time makes it possible for the Christian worshipping and adoring God in the service to feel really in union with the "Church Triumphant", the realized and completed Church in heaven. We are, in fact, often reminded of this in the Mass, nowhere more than in the Preface to the Great Prayer and in the significant reference to the heavenly altar in the *Supplices Te Rogamus*. This is a biblical truth which a particular theological development emphasized during the Middle Ages and popularized through Church art has tended to obscure. But if we go back to the New Testament we find that it is the risen Lord who is uppermost in the minds of the community at worship. This is particularly emphasized in Hebrews, the most liturgical of all New-Testament writings. Here the worship which is carried out on earth is a kind of shadow or reflection of the true worship in heaven. Christ at the right hand of God is the Minister, *leitourgos*, of the true Tabernacle, and in this worship he is assisted by the whole of the heavenly court. This comes through in an even more striking way in the Apocalypse, which is organized round the idea of the heavenly liturgy as the final goal of our worship here on earth and which ends, as does Paul's Corinthian letter, with the ardent cry for the Lord's speedy coming.[1] This idea of the correspondence between the heavenly and the earthly worship may lie behind Paul's rather strange reference to the angels on account

---

[1] 16.22; Apoc. 22.20.

8

of whose presence women ought to keep their heads covered during the service.[1] The forward looking, the anxious scanning of the horizon, the joy and ardent longing are there on every page.

This joy in worship is something which we have to some extent lost and which we must recover. The joy in the Spirit, in the use of his gifts—even with all the reservations which we have to make in their regard—still conveys powerfully what living the new life meant to the Corinthian Christians. There was no need for a calendar of feast-days and saints' days apart from those which commemorated the great act of salvation; every day was a feast-day for those to whom faith had brought what the First Epistle of Peter calls "the unspeakable joy".[2] This *gaudium immensum atque probum* which permeated life in these early Churches was directly connected with the consciousness of belonging to the holy, redeemed community of the last age, as is clear from what Paul says to the Church at Salonika where this expectation ran especially high: "Rejoice always, pray constantly, given thanks in all circumstances

[1] 1 Cor. 11.10. See Delling, p. 45, *n.* 2.
[2] 1,8. The early Christian expression of this can be seen in the designation *feria* (feast-day) given to each day as a liturgical unit. This impression has been weakened by a too luxuriant overgrowth of saints' days.

... do not quench the Spirit."[1] In spite of appearances to the contrary, in spite of the long road we have come, the same word holds good for us today.

[1] 1 Thess. 5.16–19; cf. Phil. 4.4–5: "Rejoice in the Lord always; again I will say, Rejoice. Let all men know your forbearance. The Lord is at hand."

APPENDIX 1

PAUL AT ATHENS
(Acts 17.16–34)

THIS chapter of Acts which describes Paul's visit to Athens and the discourse which he made there claims our attention in relation to our reading of 1 Corinthians, since it provides us with a special case of his becoming "all things to all men". (1 Cor. 9.22.) We see him attempting to build a bridge across the chasm between the Church and the secular mind on the level of ideas, and in so doing he gives us an excellent example of how such an attempt should be carried through. This is an invaluable complement to Paul's teaching on the meaning of Church membership in 1 Corinthians, since we might easily get an impression of exclusiveness and distance from his letter and from other passages in his correspondence where he gives great emphasis to the failure of natural man and of the potentialities of secular existence.

Paul's presence in Athens in the first place was, as we have seen, something of an accident, and his meeting with Stoic and Epicurean philosophers rather a chance encounter. For the author of Acts, however, it was an encounter full of significance.

Luke begins his story in Jerusalem and ends it in Rome; here in Athens we are at the mid-point, the heart of philosophical paganism even in Paul's day when it was some centuries past its best. Luke invests this meeting between the urbane, rather *blasé* representatives of an ascendant philosophy and the unprepossessing Jew, the "babbler" from Asia Minor, with great significance. It was for him a clash between two worlds; one anthropocentric, concerned with the problem of man in his here-and-now existence, the heir of a great philosophical tradition; the other theocentric, occupied only with God's call from beyond the sense world, as revealed in the Scriptures. It was the first time that we know of, though by no means the last, when Christianity would be called upon *as a religion* to give an account of itself and to answer the questions which any religion or philosophy has to answer.

The circumstances for making such an attempt at that moment were not particularly favourable. We are told that, on viewing the many statues in that city in which, as Petronius drily remarked, it was easier to meet a god than a man, "his spirit was provoked within him".[1] We recall his violent reaction some time before at Lystra when the crowd wanted to sacrifice to him and Barnabas and how, writing to the Roman Church at a later

[1] Acts 17.16; Luke uses the verb *paroxyno*—almost "to be in a paroxysm of anger".

date, he was to paint such a dark picture of pagan religion and the moral corruption which, for Paul, went with it.[1] That there was little goodwill on the part of his hearers can be detected in the thinly disguised irony of their questions: "What would this babbler say?", "May we know what this new teaching is?..." For them he was evidently just one more peddlar of strange gods and goddesses from the East—in this case Jesus and Anastasis, understood very likely by them as the goddess Resurrection.[2] It is only when we bear this in mind that we can appreciate the courage and resource shown by Paul in this unique missionary effort on the intellectual level.

Before going on to the discourse itself there is the question of authenticity, whether Paul did in fact make such an attempt. This is part of a wider problem in Acts for which the reader will have to be referred to the commentaries. Suffice it to say that, with the majority of scholars today, we can with a clear conscience accept Harnack's arguments as against Norden for substantial authenticity, while at the same time not expecting too much. Luke had no intention here or elsewhere of providing us with anything like an exact

[1] Acts 14.14; Rom. 1.22–32.

[2] *Anastasis* is feminine in Greek. It was customary for deities to be in pairs; we recall Simon Magus and his deified consort Helena.

transcription of a tape-recording of what Paul said.

We should note how Paul undertook this dialogue (it was meant to be that)—with sympathy, determined to go as far as he could with his hearers; this he did not by making a series of concessions but by being always open, always anxious to find points of contact and overlap. He begins with the familiar *captatio benevolentiae*, congratulating them on the religious sentiment evidenced in the city by the many if sometimes ambiguous signs of worship. There is more to this introductory compliment than a useful manoeuvre or a literary device; the *daimonoi*, the Powers beyond, haunted Greek thought even in periods of the most assertive rationalism; at no time was this more evident than in that uneasy century which lies between the composition of the Book of Wisdom and the appearance of Paul in Athens, a period during which both Stoics and Epicureans were turning to a powerful if sometimes vague religious, pantheistic mysticism. One has only to read the *De Rerum Natura* of Lucretius relevant to the scene in Athens since Lucretius was an Epicurean and quotes the Stoic Aratus as Paul does here, to see how all that age down through the early years of the Empire was remarkably similar to our own. It comes through very well for the modern reader in Thornton Wilder's brilliant historical reconstruction in *The Ides of*

March. Paul was aware of all this and so decided to ignore the insults and cynicism and try to establish contact with that religious undercurrent and see where such a contact would lead him.

From this point, the whole discourse is a good example of how to enter into religious dialogue, which always degenerates into a *dialogue des sourds* so long as the participants remain within their own frontiers, use their own categories of thought, which are often unintelligible to others, and decide in advance that they must at all costs defend themselves from the others. In Paul's contribution there is, first of all, a conspicuous lack of Scripture quotation, though there are, naturally enough, echoes of biblical language; on the contrary, he takes care to quote only Stoic poets and lines which would be familiar to his audience. He takes his point of departure from something within the field of his listeners' experience, an *ex-voto* statue to an unknown god which had caught his eye[1]—and goes on from there to a kind of discussion entirely familiar in Stoic and Epicurean circles: the nature and

[1] There is good supporting evidence for the custom of building altars with this inscription or one similar, e.g., in Pausanias (c. A.D. 150–200) and the contemporary Apollonius of Tyana; there is also the much discussed Pergamum inscription. Epimenides, quoted here by Paul, is reported to have cleared Athens of plague by recommending altars to unknown gods.

attributes of the Deity, the question of nature and providence, the theology of history—and only then after a careful preparation of the ground does he introduce what is essential and irreducible in the Christian faith. Until he came to the Resurrection and the call to action—the Pauline *Now*—it is unlikely that his audience would have found anything to disagree with.

The quotations are significant. In speaking of the nearness of God to natural man in the world he recalls a verse of the poem on the Minos written by the Cretan Epimenides, the half-legendary figure of the sixth century before Christ. This was dear to the Stoics, who applied it to man's life in union with nature, in the cosmos conceived of as a divine organism into which man is absorbed in death. It illustrates the Stoic de-mythologizing of the old stories of gods and goddesses, since the poem seems to have been directed against the Cretans who claimed to have Zeus' tomb, a claim which the poet denounced as a lie since Zeus, the Living One, could not die.[1] This view fitted in well with the Stoic theory on the Deity and their feeling for the divine immanence in the world of nature, and it is this which Paul tries to go along with in order to keep his hearers with him and lead them to the *dénouement*. The

[1] It seems likely that another verse of the same poem is quoted in Titus 1.12. The name Zeus is, of course, derived from *zao*, "to live".

snatch about men being the offspring of God is taken from Aratus, a Stoic and fellow countryman of Paul, whose *Phaenomena* seem to have been in vogue about that time, having been translated by Cicero and commented by several writers, Stoic and otherwise. Thus Paul was able to create a climate in which discussion should have been possible.

But the rapprochement was not just on the superficial level of quoting the other side's writers and picking up some of their catch-phrases. It involved a real attempt to penetrate the thought of these men, which was the dominant thought of that age, in order to find at what point the irreducible fact, the unique Christian event, could be inserted. His opening polemic against a purely material cult is a case in point, since it provided a fortunate coincidence between scriptural revelation, as taken up in that period frequently by Jewish Dispersion religious writers,[1] and the thought of the age as represented by the Stoics in particular. We find the same thing also in the visit to Athens of the Pythagorean sage Apollonius, a fact which Norden made much of in arguing his case of inauthenticity.

The same thing comes out even more clearly when Paul moves on from the nature of worship

[1] See, a century earlier, in the Book of Wisdom. The polemic against "temples made with hands" occurs in a different context in Stephen's speech, Acts 7.48.

to the nature of the God who was the object of worship. It was connatural for Paul, whose whole mental world was based on the revealed word, to think of God as a Person beyond the world of nature. According to Stoic teaching, however, God is in and of the world conceived of as one organic, living whole; in fact, the two terms were convertible.[1] To put it more precisely, God was thought of as the active principle of reality of which inert matter was the passive counterpart. He was for them, to use an expression coined by Paul Tillich, the true "ground of being". Paul does not reject the spiritual insight in this doctrine; on the contrary, at the head of a long line of Christian thinkers, including St Augustine, he takes over the basic truth in the doctrine of divine immanence. When he begins by saying: "What you worship as unknown, *this* I proclaim to you" he is referring to the divine nature as such, and from then on he tries to follow through along this perspective. It is significant in this respect that only here do we find Paul using the term *theion*, the Divine, the Deity[2]; he uses it as in keeping with

[1] Cicero tells us: "Cleanthes tum ipsum mundum Deum dicit esse, tum totius naturae menti atque animo tribuit hoc nomen, tum ultimum ... atque complexum ardorem qui aether nominatur certissimum Deum iudicat."

[2] Acts 17.29; in 27 the Western text (D) reads *theion* for *theon*.

the Stoic teaching on the divine immanence, the principle which pervades the whole universe and also therefore the human mind.

What is remarkable and significant in all this is that Paul starts here, with the Stoics and the trend in contemporary spirituality, from man's movement towards God, not vice versa. Throughout all his epistles what is uppermost is the divine movement towards us in Jesus, the divine initiative—God makes the first move: "God shows his love for us in that while we were yet sinners Christ died for us." (Rom. 5.8–9.) Here, and only rarely elsewhere in Paul, we feel the movement of the whole creation, recapitulated in man, in its yearning for completion in God, which is heard like a vast sigh throughout the cosmos.[1] For if it is true that man receives his call from beyond nature, it is equally certain that he is himself part of nature, knit into the complex fabric of the universe, and that in consequence the destiny of the universe is involved deeply in that of man. While the Stoics expressed this by the correspondence between the *anima mundi* and the *anima humana*, we might think today in terms of teleological evolution and man's place in nature, a subject so much discussed in recent years.

[1] Cf. Rom. 8.19–23 and his teaching on the *pleroma* and the destiny of the universe in Ephesians and Colossians in particular.

From this point, Paul goes on to a thumbnail sketch of the theology of history. God is the source of all good in creation; his providence directs all human affairs. Here again this finds echo in the highly developed Stoic teaching on the divine *pronoia* or providence, which is behind the apparently fortuitous succession of historical events and personal vicissitudes. Each nation is allotted its sphere and given its destiny which has to be followed out within the fixed time allotted to it. There is even here the basic Stoic tenet of the unity of the human family: "He made from one every nation of men to live on all the face of the earth"[1]—a doctrine which was the starting-point for the idea of universal brotherhood preached by many Stoic philosophers, an idea which recurs often in Paul's letters if within a rather different perspective.

But the question arises: Where is history leading? Has it a goal in the future or has it already reached its goal? Is there any possibility of a radically new and original event within the space-time dimension? For his hearers such a question could have had little meaning; even if for the Stoics this world order, this present age, was destined to end catastrophically in fire, it was only so that another world order identical to this should rise in its stead, and so it would go on.

[1] Acts 17.26; the Western text reads, "he made of one blood . . . ".

At this point Paul had to insert the unique experience afforded by the Christian faith—Jesus risen from the dead, Jesus lord of history, Jesus whose coming as judge of the living and the dead was the object of Christian faith and hope. He did so in the most universal and least specifically Jewish way possible: there is nothing of the role of the Chosen People in the history of salvation, nothing of the miracles, the death on the Cross, the founding of a society. God has appointed *a man* through whom the future judgement is to take place, a man who was dead and is now alive.

It was at this point that his hearers stopped listening; the one or two who "joined him and believed" were a small recompense for that magnificent effort at comprehension and transposition. That this failure affected Paul deeply we may gather from the tone of the opening chapters of the Letter to the Corinthians and the description he gives of his state of mind when he arrived there from Athens:

When I came to you, brethren, I did not come proclaiming to you the testimony of God in lofty words or wisdom. For I decided to know nothing among you except Jesus Christ and him crucified. And I was with you in weakness and in much fear and trembling; and my speech and my message were not in plausible words of wisdom, but in demonstration of the

Spirit and power, that your faith might not rest
in the wisdom of men but in the power of God.
[2.1–5.]

This represented a perfectly natural revulsion of
feeling and is a permanent warning against a false
alignment of the Word of God, the Word from
beyond, with any self-contained philosophical
system. But Paul's discourse remains as a magnificent example of missionary method at a deep
level, the level of the mind and the heart.

APPENDIX 2

1 CORINTHIANS IN THE CHURCH'S LITURGICAL CYCLE

IT might be taken as an indication of the need for Scripture reading in private or, better still, in a group, outside the liturgical service, that of the 437 verses in this letter less than a sixth are read at Mass in the course of the liturgical cycle. There is the thanksgiving at the beginning, a bit of Paul's personal *apologia*, the tail-end of the passage dealing with the immoral Christian, the passage in the idiom of sport and the Old-Testament homily with its notorious preacher's headache of the Israelites drinking from the Rock which followed them. There is also, of course, the eucharistic passage (twice), the chapter dealing with the charismatic gifts and the need for charity, and the Pauline *kerygma* of ch. 15. Despite the fact that, after Romans, 1 Corinthians is the most frequently used of Paul's Epistles in the Liturgy, anyone who studies the letter with the help provided in the foregoing chapters will see how much valuable material is not represented. Hence the value of a more integral study of Paul's thought.

We give here for convenience the liturgical occurrence of passages from this letter.

4th Sunday in Advent	Paul's *apologia*	4.1–5
Septuagesima Sunday	Paul's example; O.T. homily	9.24–7; 10.1–5
Quinquagesima Sunday	Love	13.1–13
Maundy Thursday	The Lord's Supper	11.20–32
Easter Sunday	The Passover	5.7–8
Corpus Christi	The Lord's Supper	11.23–9
9th Sunday after Pentecost	O.T. Homily (continued)	10.6–13
10th Sunday after Pentecost	Charismatic Gifts	12.2–11
11th Sunday after Pentecost	Resurrection	15.1–10
18th Sunday after Pentecost	Thanksgiving	1.4–8

APPENDIX 3

READING GUIDE TO 1 CORINTHIANS

A

1.1–3	Greeting
4–9	Thanksgiving

B

1.10–16	"Schisms" in the community
1.17–2.16	First reason: a false "philosophy" of the Christian life
3.1–4	Second reason: their spiritual immaturity
4–15	The question of allegiance to Paul or Apollos
16–23	*Argumentum ad hominem*
4.1–21	Third reason: their pride and arrogance

C

Paul's reaction to news which had reached him from Corinth

5.1–13	The incestuous Christian
6.1–8	Taking fellow Christians to law
9–11	A solemn warning
12–20	Fornication (connected with pagan ritual)

D

Cases of conscience put to him

E

Within the Liturgical Service

APPENDIX 4

SUGGESTIONS FOR FURTHER THEMATIC READING IN THE NEW-TESTAMENT LETTERS TO EARLY CHURCHES

---

1. *The Christian's Vocation in the Church*

Rom. 1.18–32	The failure of natural man
Col. 1.24–9	Christian wisdom
Rom. 8.1–17	Christian existence in the Church; the destiny of creation
Eph. 1.3–14	What it means to be a Christian
2 Cor. 3.4–18	The Old and the New Dispensations

2. *Church Unity*

Eph. 4.1–24	The unity of the Faith
Col. 1.15–23	Unity of the world and unity of the Church in Christ
Phil. 2.1–11	Necessity of selflessness for unity
1 John 4.7–21	Love of God, love of the neighbour basic to unity

3. *Authority and Hierarchy*

Rom. 13.1–7	Attitude to secular authority
Heb. 2.5–9	The God-given supremacy of man in the universe
2 Cor. 6.3–13	The true minister

Rom. 12.3–8	Humble use of God's gifts in the Church
1 Thess. 2.1–12	Spiritual paternity

4. *Sacramental Life in the Church*

Eph. 3.7–19	The Christian mystery
Rom. 6.1–11	The meaning of baptism
Rom. 5.1–5	Strength from the Spirit for the Christian life
Heb. 6.4–8; John 2.1–6	Fear and confidence in the sacrament of penance
Heb. 9.11–22	The one sacrifice of the New Covenant
Heb. 5.1–10	Christ the eternal high priest
Jas. 5.13–20	Anointing of the sick and other charitable ministries
Eph. 5.22–33	The mystery of Christian Matrimony

5. *Morality and Maturity*

Gal. 5.13–25	Christian liberty
Col. 3.1–17	The risen life of the Christian
Eph. 5.1–20	Moral norms
2 Tim. 2.1–7	Christian asceticism
Titus 2.11–14	Moral life under the sign of the Lord's coming

6. *The Redeemed Body*

1 Tim. 4.1–5	Rejection of a false dualism
1 Thess. 4.1–8	Sanctification through purity
Gal. 5.16–26	The law of the Spirit
1 Peter 3.1–7	Advice to wives and husbands

7. *Liturgy and Life*

Heb. 10.1–25	Christ minister of the heavenly liturgy
Eph. 2.11–22	The community of the New Covenant in the blood of Christ
Phil. 4.4–7	Christian joy
1 Peter 2.4–10	The universal priesthood of the faithful.

INDEX OF NAMES AND SUBJECTS

INDEX OF SCRIPTURE REFERENCES